Hellenismos Today

By Timothy Jay Alexander

FIRST EDITION

Published by Lulu

ISBN 978-1-4303-1427-1

Do not say a little in many words but a great deal in a few.

~ Pythagoras ~

This book is dedicated to
Emperor Julian (Flavius Claudius Iulianus)
Last Pagan Emperor of Rome

Contents

Introduction

THIS BOOK IS about a modern religious practice and is not being presented as a history lesson. Hellenismos, sometimes called Hellenic Polytheistic Reconstructionism or Hellenic Reconstructionism, is a modern religion which draws from the past to rebuild what was lost. We attempt to be as authentic as possible to the ancient religion of Greece without losing sight of the fact more than 1500 years separate us from the ancients.

This book is intended to serve as a guide and introduction into the practice of Hellenismos, the polytheistic Reconstructionist religion which honors the Gods of ancient Greece. Within these pages the reader will find useful information introducing them to this modern religion, and enough information to begin a personal practice. No initiation or formal conversion is necessary, just an open heart and a willingness to honor the old Gods.

Practitioners of Reconstructionist religions, not just Hellenismos, are often perceived as being very academic, rigid or even dogmatic because of an insistence of making historically accurate statements, and their practice of scholarly study to rebuild an ancient religion in a modern context. Hellenismos is not a reenactment group. It is not role playing. This is about modern religious worship and spirituality, and about respectfully and devoutly honoring the ancient Greek Gods in a way that embraces the past without losing sight of the fact that we live in the 21st century.

As a book about a modern religion, this is not intended to be an academic source, discussion, or debate about history. I believe that anyone interested in learning about Hellenismos initially wants to know how believers are practicing today, not necessarily how religion was practiced in the 2nd century BCE. I will do my best when discussing my religion to keep it in a modern context, but there is simply no way to discuss Hellenismos without making historical references. I have one chapter dedicated to history but beyond that I will only make, when appropriate, easily verifiable historical references to help place certain concepts and practices in context.

There is also a presumption made the reader has at least a basic understanding of who the ancient Greeks were. You should have an idea, at the very least, of Greece's geographical location, of some of the city-states like Athens and Sparta, of historical figures such as Alexander, Plato, and Hesiod, and be familiar with the Greek Gods and their mythologies.

An attempt has been made to provide the reader with enough information to, at the very least, begin a practice of personal devotion, but it is recommended one invests the time in doing additional research to learn as much as they can about both the Ancient Greek religion and the modern practice of Hellenismos.

Learning the ancient Greek language is very important to many practitioners of Hellenismos. It's not to me, and as you read through this book I have limited my use of Greek words to the bare essentials. I thoroughly understand many of the reasons my colleagues give for finding it an essential part of their practice. I accept completely that it is a devotional act that has great meaning to them. As I studied the ancient Greek religion there is one glaring fact that jumped out at me, and that is all religion is local. I am an American, living in Pennsylvania, and I speak English. Its not that I don't see value in it for those that do it, it just doesn't hold the same value for me.

It should also be noted that many identify Hellenismos as a Pagan religion, including myself. I will be refraining from using the word Pagan to describe the religion going forward. The simple fact is many within Hellenismos find the word's use as defamatory. The word Pagan, though embraced as a form of empowerment today by many, was originally a derogatory term used by Christians to insult practitioners of the old ways.

Pagan comes from the Latin word *paganus*, meaning "rural", "rustic" or "of the country." *Paganus* was used in ancient times to mean "country dweller" or "villager." After Emperor Constantine made Christianity the state religion of Rome, Christianity spread more slowly throughout the countryside than it did within the cities. The word for "country dweller" began to be used to describe any person who was "not a Christian." The word was transformed to pagan after being adopted by Middle English-speaking Christians. It was used as a slur to imply that rustic areas where either to stupid or too uncivilized to embrace Christianity.

I hope that sections of this book do not come across as Christian bashing, but we should not whitewash the facts of the matter when it comes to Christian dominance in the West. In the 4th century CE the Emperor Constantine, in an attempt to reunite a dying Empire, made Christianity the official state religion of Rome; he then began ordering the destruction of temples in the Hellenic world. By the end of the 5th century all the temples in Athens, Olympia, and other Greek city-states had been sacked, and in Egypt the philosopher Hypatia was burned with her books by the local Bishop. Every indigenous people that Christianity encountered, from the Celts to the Norse, from the African tribes to the First Nation peoples in America, were forcibly converted. Those they could not convert through evangelizing were converted by the sword; those that could not be converted by the sword were killed. Once converted to Christianity, every possible attempt was made to strip these people of their cultural heritage. There are scholars and theologians who make the claim that monotheism is the natural progression of religious and spiritual consciousness. I don't see anything natural about it. These are the facts, and they are undisputable.

Hellenismos is a rapidly growing religion. I have repeatedly come across people who read something I wrote, were motivated then to seek out more information, and in no time they were devout enthusiastic practitioners. Hellenismos is the kind of religion that embraces humanity and works for its development. It is a practical religion that embraces the individual and challenges them to be the very best they can be in all aspects of their life without the harsh judgments and dogmatism of some more mainstream religions. Our Gods acknowledge our existence and take an active interest in our lives. I hope that while reading this book you are able to get a true sense of what an absolutely beautiful, energizing, and liberating religion Hellenismos is.

Polytheistic Reconstructionism

POLYTHEISTIC RECONSTRUCTIONISM, SOMETIMES simply referred to as Reconstructionism, is the practice of rebuilding an ancient cultural pre-Christian religion based on the best available archaeological evidence and, where evidence is lacking, making inferences from scholarly comparisons to similar cultures and religions both ancient and modern.

Reconstructionist religions tend, more often then not, to have certain unique identifying markers. They stress scholarly research, which means using primary and secondary sources in addition to other academic materials. Religions which are Reconstructionist make a clear distinction between Unverified Personal Gnosis (also called UPG, spiritual knowledge gained through personal experience) and historically accurate information. Most Reconstructionist religions will also be identifiable as "hard polytheists", believing the Gods to be individual and distinct spiritual beings.

The distinction between hard and soft polytheists is a relatively new concept. The ideas evolved from Neopagans, practicing a completely modern religion, identifying themselves as polytheists yet still believing in a single ultimate deity. The concept that a religion professing a single deity could still be polytheist evolved from the Wiccan concept that all Goddesses are one Goddess, all Gods are one God, and the Goddess and the God are each aspects of a single ultimate being. In soft polytheism, the Gods are not believed to be individual and distinct beings, but that they are aspects, interpretations, or manifestations of a single deity.

Hellenismos is not the only Polytheistic Reconstructionist religion. The first publicly visible religion with this distinction was Asatru (a religion attempting to revive the ancient Nordic religion), beginning in the late 60s and touted itself as "the religion with homework." Other forms of Polytheistic Reconstructionism include Celtic Reconstructionism based on Celtic cultures, Religio Romana based on pre-Christian Rome, Romuva based on Lithuania's ethnic traditions, and many others.

We do, though, have to give credit where credit is due. While there seems to be a level of tension between some Reconstructionists and Neopagan groups such as Wicca and Modern Druidry, Reconstructionism has to acknowledge those pioneering individuals like Gerald Gardner, founder of the Gardnerian Tradition of Wicca in the early half of the twentieth century, for paving the way for our movements and reviving interest in the ancient divinities. If it were not for the work of Gerald Gardner and others like him, we would not have the level of acceptance that we do today.

Tension between Reconstructionists and groups like Wicca and Modern Druidry come, at times, as a result from our perceptions of the Gods, how groups interact with the Gods, and validity of historical claims. Reconstructionists see many Neopagans taking the Gods from the particular ancient cultural religion out of context and reducing them to a simple archetypal figure, not appreciating and respecting the individuality and complexity of the Gods. Many Neopagans are also soft polytheists and believe that the individual Gods and Goddesses are ultimately manifestations of a single ultimate deity. Typically, a Reconstructionist is defined as a hard polytheist, believing each of the Gods and Goddesses are distinct even if the perception is sometimes tampered with the pantheistic view that the Gods exist at a level of Unity with an Ultimate Source. The big issue though seems to be how Neopagans interact with the ancient Gods. How it is sometimes described by some Neopagans that they "use" the Gods in spellcraft and magick or that they "bind" a God to do their will is seen as extremely impious and disrespectful to many Reconstructionists, very often a violation of their ethical codes and moral standards.

Historical claims are also a point of contention between Reconstructionists and some Neopagans. One example of this is the unsubstantiated claim that there had once existed an ancient global

Goddess monotheism with a female ruled utopia. I have even read rewrites of ancient myths done in a way to imply that the ancients subscribed to the contemporary concept that all Goddesses are one Goddess and all Gods are one God. This sort of fabrication or rewriting of history is called "fakelore" and is not an acceptable practice among Reconstructionists.

Fakelore is either the complete fabrication of lore, legends, and myths or the reworking of original texts to meet specific sensibilities. The act of creating or rewriting stories does not in and of itself give a work this negative connotation, but it is the presentation of a completely original story or a revision as being authentically historical (either directly or through omission) that defines real fakelore. Reconstructionists often expand this definition to include any unsubstantiated or fictitious historical claim created (intentionally or otherwise) to misrepresent an ancient culture, religious practice, or ancient belief.

I want to take a moment here to expand on the two phrases hard polytheist and soft polytheist. Hard polytheism is the belief that each God or Goddess is a distinct individual being completely separate and independent from all others. Soft polytheism believes that each of the individual Gods and Goddesses are separate manifestations of a single divine being. Hard polytheists rarely take the most extreme stance that each God and Goddess is absolutely individual and will blend their beliefs with a somewhat pantheistic philosophy. They will often accept as true that while the Gods and Goddesses are distinct individual beings they exist in Unity with a Divine Source, an impersonal self-sustaining force from which all things emanate. Soft polytheism presumes that each of the individual Gods and Goddesses are separate manifestations of a single divine being and will take a more monotheistic approach.

One criticism of Reconstructionism is a perceived rigidity caused by their commitment to scholarly study, to making accurate claims when discussing the history of their religion, and often aggressively challenging blatantly false historical statements about the ancient culture which their modern practice has derived. I have to be clear here, Reconstructionist religions are not the ancient religions themselves. They are modern religions based on ancient cultures and their spiritual practices, just as Christian religions are modern religions based on the 2000 year old teachings of a carpenter from Nazareth. Scholarly study for many

Reconstructionists is an act of personal devotion that brings them closer to their Gods, not simple cold academia.

One of the difficulties of attempting to recreate the practices of ancient religions, aside from sometimes lacking source material, is that it can be difficult to discern what was religious and what was not. While most ancient cultures would not be considered theocracies by today's standards, spirituality was so intertwined with everyday living there is often no absolute distinction between secular and spiritual. Religious practice was just a matter of fact with most ancient peoples.

A Reconstructionists path is not as difficult or complicated as all the talk of historical accuracy and scholarly study make it sound. Hellenic Reconstructionism focuses primarily on the "public" or (sometimes called) "popular" religion of ancient Greece. This means the religious calendar, the public festivals, the role of "typical" priests and priestesses, and the religious life of the everyday Greek. Philosophy was the bastion of the intellectual elite. While a Reconstructionist may draw from philosophy, it did exist outside the "public" religion. Mystery cults, again the stronghold of the few, were secretive and initiatory with little surviving evidence, and again outside the scope of the "public" religion.

Polytheistic Reconstructionism is still a young and growing group of religious movements, but I believe based on my own personal observations that in democratic countries with secular governments where freedom of religion is granted, polytheistic religions will grow once again to be a dominant form of worship. It is in cultures where a strict hierarchal system exists and absolute rule is granted to one individual, such as feudal systems, that monotheistic religions flourish through rigid authoritarianism.

Ancient Greek Religion

HELLENISMOS IS A term first coined by Emperor Julian (Flavius Claudius Iulianus) who is sometimes referred to as the Last Pagan Emperor of Rome. He ruled the Roman Empire from 331-363 CE. Emperor Julian was a philosopher who attempted to restore worship of the ancient Gods using a form of Neo-Platonism. Many Hellenic Reconstructionists honor Emperor Julian as a Hero, and it is through his example that we are attempting to revive the recognition and worship of the ancient Greek Gods.

Unlike revealed religions (Christianity and Wicca are two examples) the ancient Greek religion has no firm beginning. It fades back into early human history and can not be attested to the teaching of a single man or group. Early cultures' rites principally centered on the honoring of animals hunted and the appeasing of spirits. As societies began to develop the focus changed to agriculture and fertility Gods. Over time civilizations became even more complex as city-states rose and the Gods and Goddesses began to be recognized for their governances of complex human behavior.

The Greek religion gets its "official" start with the Minoan civilization of Crete and the early mainland Greece settlements dating somewhere between the 7th and 4th millennium BCE. It was once believed that the Minoan religion was unified and based on the worship of a mother Goddess, but current archaeological evidence has proven that not to be true. The practices during this time where, most often, outdoor ceremonies that included dance, offerings, and sacrifices.

The Mycenaean religion, from the Late Helladic period (2nd millennium BCE), is considered to be a continuation of the Minoan. This time is often the setting of the great epics from Homer and much of Greek mythology. The religion is definitely polytheistic and we begin to find many names of well-known Gods including Zeus, Poseidon, and Dionysus. While there are differences in ritual and belief between the Mycenaean religion and the Classical religion of Greece, there are many similarities including offerings and animal sacrifices.

A short period from approximately 1050 BCE to 750 BCE marks Greece's movement from the Bronze to Iron Age, and is named the Dark Age. Curiously, little is known about this period in Greek history. While specific evidence is minimal, it is believed that this period also marks the creation of the Classical religion from the Minoan and Mycenaean with a suspected heavy influence from Near East cultures.

The 5th and 4th century BCE is defined as Greece's Classical Age. It is the period when the pantheon we know today truly took shape; the mythologies creating their hierarchal structure and their interpersonal relationships were recognized. Many localities and city-states had their own version of accounts. At this time more complex forms of worship developed including hymns, prayers, vows, votive offerings and sacrifices. Athens took the lead role in Greece during this era.

The Hellenistic period begins with Alexander in 336 BCE. For modern practitioners of Hellenismos, very often the focus is to base their practice on this period of ancient Greek history. Here is when philosophy augmented religious expression among the educated elite, yet the Classical religious practices thrived as a public expression. It is during this time that we believe that myth lost its recognition as literal truth and became perceived as allegories of greater knowledge. This period of ever increasing enlightenment ended when Christianity became the state religion of Rome, Greek temples were ordered sacked, priests and philosophers were slaughtered.

I have come to the opinion that the worship of the Gods seems to be reflective of how a society is organized not necessarily a culture's level of development. Smaller, more clan or tribal societies, keep very close to earth spirits such as totems and ancestor worship. Cultures that are larger and broader in scope recognize more complex pantheons. Peoples existing in feudal systems with strict hierarchies, where absolute authority is granted to one person, succumb to monotheism. This observation has led me to the personal conclusion that in democratic countries, with secular governments where freedom of religion is granted, polytheistic religions will again grow to be a dominant form of worship.

Hellenic Reconstructionism allows for a great deal of diversity in beliefs and practice because of the very nature of ancient Greece. The ancient Greek religion included the different practices of the various city-states, the varied concepts of the different philosophers and philosophical schools, the mystery cults, and the many acts of personal devotion.

We have as the primary focus the "public" or "popular" religion which included the temples, festivals, and other public events. Each city-state had a unique religious calendar. They had their own versions of the myths. The practices of each city-state could almost be described as separate denominations or even religions.

We have the philosophers, their concepts of the universe and their perceptions of the Gods and the Gods' roles. These philosophers still influence society today; their names are often household words. We have Plato, the founder of the Academy in Athens. There is Aristotle, student of Plato and teacher to Alexander. Pythagoras, who is best known today as the father of modern mathematics, was an astronomer, mathematician, and philosopher who founded the Pythagorean movement. These are just three of the best known philosophers. Ancient Greece has a wealth of spiritual knowledge available from a multitude of teachers, and that is just what survived the ravages of Christianity and time.

We also look to the cults. Please, let's not confuse the ancient cults of Greece with the destructive cults sometimes found in modern society. A cult is simply a group of people worshiping outside the mainstream. As we look at the Greeks, mainstream would be classified as the "public" or "popular" religion of the city-states, while the cults focused oftentimes on exploring the mysteries associated with a single divinity. These cults were often initiatory and secretive; as a result few records remain. Practice of mystery traditions is some times looked at as outside a Hellenic Reconstructionist practice, but since there are no set hard fast rules barring the practice some Reconstructionists may choose to explore these mysteries.

Personal acts of devotion are, I believe, at the heart of ancient Greek practice and as a result at the heart of modern Hellenismos. The ancient Greeks had no word for religion; the reason for this was because spirituality and acts of devotion where so interwoven into everyday life that it was all very a matter of fact. Anyone could make offerings to the Gods. Anyone could petition the Gods. Most rites of passage such as welcoming ceremonies, weddings, and funerals were handled by the family. No priest or priestess stood between worshipers and the Gods.

All this being said the ancient Greeks, with all their diversity in thought and practice, were very much defined by being Greek and the Greek ways of doing and thinking. Ancient Greece is labeled as being syncretic. Syncretism is the adopting of contradictory concepts and transforming them to remove philosophical conflicts. Greece did import foreign Gods, concepts, and practices, but they converted them into being uniquely Greek. This practice of syncretism is very different then the eclectic practices of the many Neopagan religions. Eclecticism technically takes diverse religious and philosophical concepts and practices in their original form, allowing for a shifting paradigm. The Greeks defined foreign cultures and practices by how Greek they perceived them. The idea of incorporating concepts which contradicted fundamental Greek beliefs and ideals was unconscionable.

As a widespread practice the ancient Greek religion ended after the Roman Emperor Constantine made Christianity Rome's state religion and ordered the destruction of many Greek temples. There was a short lived revival a few decades after Constantine's death thanks to the efforts of Emperor Julian, but the final nail came in the 10th century of the current era when the last of the Hellenes of Laconia where forced to convert to Christianity. It is thanks to the efforts of groups like the Supreme Council of Ethnikoi Hellenes in Greece and Hellenion in the United States that Hellenismos is becoming more popular and gaining recognition as a legitimate religion.

Gods and Goddesses

I INITIALLY WANTED to use this section to discuss all the Gods, their myths, and the hierarchal structure of the Gods, Daemons, Heroes, and other divinities but, as I reflected as to what to write, I realized this is an introductory guide. This section could provide little information that you most likely did not already know. The Greek Gods, despite being perceived by many in modern times as fiction, have remained prominent in our consciousness. Their myths are still taught as part of a well rounded education. Aeschylus tells us, "When one is willing and eager, the Gods join in," so I will instruct you to take the time and enthusiastically do in-depth research of the Gods, their myths, and how they were perceived by the ancient Greeks. This will create for you an informed opinion and will help you develop your beliefs. What I do want to discuss is how the Gods are perceived by modern practitioners of Hellenismos.

Most modern practitioners of Hellenismos would generally define themselves as hard polytheists. Hard polytheists rarely take the most extreme stance that each God and Goddess is absolutely individual and will blend their beliefs with a somewhat pantheistic philosophy. They will often accept as true that, while the Gods and Goddesses are distinct individual beings they exist in Unity with a Divine Source, an impersonal self-sustaining force from which all things emanated. A hard polytheist who takes this approach most likely will also see all things that exist as a product of, contained within, and a reflection of this source. Each individual entity simply exists at a different level of Unity with the Divine Source, and see our ultimate spiritual goal as complete Unification.

It is stated on the Supreme Council of Ethnikoi Hellenes website that:

"...we must reiterate what was emphasized by Sallustius, at the beginning of his work 'On Gods and the Cosmos', i.e., that those with a desire to know about the Gods need to have been educated correctly and not to have been brought up with absurd beliefs. To have a good disposition and logical composition, so that they can accordingly understand matters as well as comprehend common meanings.

The Gods are non-personal beings, possessing both knowledge and immortality. They flow unhindered through and around the whole material world and act upon it. As functionaries of the sacred Mysteries, they participate in 'eternal formation', i.e., the continuous synthesis and de-synthesis of forms. The Gods' spheres of influence do not overlap. They are responsible for the regulation of the Natural World, whose laws they serve. They act flawlessly and without retreat, do not unite into one being, are not replaced, do not cease to exist, and cannot be defeated by the appetites and expectations of impious mortals or institutions.

The Gods are free and independent entities. They are all equally Divine and are not empowered by any other being or force. They rejoice when inferior entities freely recognize their existence and bestow upon them honor and respect. They do not however need this recognition, nor do they seek it. As Gods they want nothing, they simply shape whatever they desire." [1]

The term soft polytheist describes a belief that each of the individual Gods and Goddesses are separate manifestations of a single divine being. It is a more monotheistic approach. The best example of soft polytheism is the Wiccan belief that all Goddesses are one Goddess, all Gods are one God, and the Goddess and God are both aspects of a single deity. It is very common for a soft polytheist to intermix unrelated pantheons within their practice, most often these are the Neopagan traditions such

[1] What are the Gods? (2006) In *Supreme Council of Ethnikoi Hellenes.* Retrieved April 12, 2007, from http://www.ysee.gr/index-eng.php?type=english&f=faq#14

as Wicca or Modern Druidry. Most practitioners of Hellenismos may find this approach impious to the Gods, completely rejecting the concept.

Pantheism, at its core, is the belief that all is God. It is the idea that the universe and all within it exist as a single divine being. Some liken the concept to that of a dream. When one is dreaming, everything within the dream is not only a creation of the dreamer but the dreamer themselves. So to the pantheist everyone and everything is God with no separation at all. It is not unheard of for a Hellenist to take this approach arguing that a pure pantheistic view of the universe is an evolution derived from some philosophical teachings. It does, though, remain a controversial opinion.

The Twelve Olympian Gods, known also as the Dodekatheon, are the primary deities honored in Hellenismos. There are variations in the list depending on the mythological source, but the twelve according to Hesiod include: Zeus, Hera, Poseidon, Ares, Hermes, Hephaestus, Aphrodite, Athena, Apollo, Artemis, Demeter, and Dionysus. It is understood that Hestia stepped down from her position as an Olympian Goddess, relinquishing her position to Dionysus, and that she now dwells among humankind. As a result Hestia has a special place in Hellenic practice. She is to receive a portion of every sacrifice, recognition at every rite and ritual, and receive daily observances and prayers.

The Gods also generally are viewed in groups: the Celestial Gods which include the Olympians, the Chthonic or Earth deities ruled by Hades and Persephone, and the Sea Gods governed by Poseidon. One must not succumb to contemporary thinking having the Greek Gods locked into an archetypal typecast. While the Gods may have their primary governances, they are complex beings with concerns that cover a multitude of venues. An example I often cite is the Goddess Aphrodite who today is seen as only a Goddess of romantic love and beauty. While being a Goddess of romantic love is true, she is also a Goddess of physical love, and seen as a Goddess of the sea by many seafaring coastal city-states. Sparta, Thebes, Cyprus, and other places even viewed Aphrodite as a Goddess of war. Her many epithets and titles include "Sea Born," "Killer of Men," "She Upon the Graves," "Fair Sailing," and "Ally in War" in addition to the many associated with love and beauty.

Between the Gods and humanity are recognized the Daemons, Heroes, and other divinities which are acknowledged as intermediaries to the

Gods and guiding spirits. The Christian word demon evolved from the word Daemon after, in the fourth century, Christianity became the official state religion of Rome. This is how we come up with the modern phrase "to demonize," which is what early Christian theologians, bishops, and monks did by transforming the image of these divine spirits, recognized by the Hellenic religion, into soul stealing deceivers of humanity who are at war with "the one true God."

Many also believe in what has come to be called a "personal Daemon." This divinity would be similar to a spirit guide or guardian angel recognized in other religions. It is said that Socrates had a personal Daemon that helped him from making mistakes and assisted him in divination.

One of the most honored Daemons in daily worship is the Agathosdaemon or "good spirit." This divinity was honored in the home, represented as a snake, is a divinity which provides wealth, wisdom, and luck. It is traditional to drink to or pour out a glass of wine in honor of him at every meal for he brings abundance to a family.

Understanding the Gods as complete beings, and not just simple archetypes, is an important aspect to Hellenismos and many Reconstructionist religions. The Greeks did not have a single collective of sacred texts as Christians do; they had the sum total of all ancient works, both surviving and lost. It is so very important for any practitioner and supplicant to take the time to do in-depth research of the Gods. "No man who is not willing to help himself has any right to apply to his friends, or to the Gods," said Demosthenes. One needs to read their myths and have a real understanding of how the Gods were perceived by the ancients. Creating an informed opinion is essential in developing your beliefs and understanding.

Cosmology

COSMOLOGY IS A set of beliefs about the structure of the universe and its creation. Hellenic Reconstructionists are generally defined as Emanationists. Emanationism states that no divinity specifically created the universe, but instead everything that exists was formed through a continual process of emanation from a self created Divine Source.

Practitioners of Hellenismos who assign the Universe's existence to Emanationism have what is sometimes considered a pantheistic view. The belief is that everything that exists stems from that which preceded it; that everything that exists is a product of, contained within, and a reflection of a single divine source. We can use an analogy with a tree and the Earth to describe this philosophy. The tree is a product of, contained within, and a reflection of the earth. The tree is both apart of the Earth and separate from it. A tree comes from the Earth, lives within it, lives separate from it, and will return to it (so what we are talking about is levels of Unity). A tree is formed from that which is the Earth, and shares in what the Earth is and will become. The tree is a reflection of the Earth, and the Earth is a reflection of the tree. Emanationism ascribes this relationship to the universe and the divine source, that we are products of, contained within, and a reflection of the All, the One, Divine Source.

> "[We] perceive the Cosmos to be a self-created, infinite, 'ordered and adorned' entity that arose from within itself, and that we, and everything else in existence, are but infinitely small organic parts of this entity.
>
> Our Gods are a multitude of apportioned immortal beings, self-energizing and self-sufficient 'forces', not

personalities, that inhabit this 'Unity' that gave birth to itself. They are the multiple expressions of this Unity that give substance and order to the Cosmos and keep it interconnected and harmonious." [2]

"Unity cannot exist without the presupposition of the 'many'. The term is misleading because it has nothing to do with the number of Gods per se, but rather the placing of the Creative Cause outside the Cosmos, which in turn implies its creation from naught (a completely unscientific thesis). Monotheists believe that the laws governing the Universe emanate from the only external, eternal being. This justifies the 'Creator's' right to act autocratically towards 'his' own creation, which has a beginning and will die at some time, as per 'his' desire.

In contrast, the ethnic polytheistic religions assert that the living Cosmos has emanated from within itself and is eternal. There is no external 'Cause' that created all from nothing. The Gods are self-reliant and conscious forces, who are multiple expressions of Unity, emanate from within it and serve its perpetual path." [3]

Emanationists will also sometimes refer to the fractals in nature as examples of their philosophy. A fractal is a geometric shape that can be subdivided, and each segment is then a reduced copy of the whole. A tree, again, is a good natural example of a fractal, with each branch and offshoot being a reduced copy of the whole. Fractals are everywhere in nature and include clouds, snow flakes, mountains, rivers, and our own system of blood vessels. I have even heard fractals described many times as the thumbprint of God.

There are also those with a competing idea. A synthesis of Creationism and Emanationism in which it is believed a single divine source emanated the Gods. The Gods then created the mundane universe from *prima*

---

[2] What are your beliefs and what is your Religion called? (2006) In *Supreme Council of Ethnikoi Hellenes*. Retrieved April 12, 2007, from http://www.ysee.gr/index-eng.php?type=english&f=faq#13

[3] Are you therefore Polytheists? (2006) In *Supreme Council of Ethnikoi Hellenes*. Retrieved April 12, 2007, from http://www.ysee.gr/index-eng.php?type=english&f=faq#19

materia, a formless primordial substance that is the basis of all matter. Many of those who adopt this philosophical approach will point to quantum physics, M-theory, and Strings to coincide with the perception that the universe was created using a primal material.

Hellenic Reconstructionists realize no matter which philosophical idea they generally subscribe, no matter how the world came into being, it did so in a natural and in a scientifically explainable way. With all the discussing and debating that goes on in the Hellenic Reconstructionist community, this issue is almost universally left alone because of the understanding that the universe exists naturally and functions in a scientifically explainable way.

> "[The] Hellenic religion… is non-dogmatic, naturalistic, polytheistic, clearly defined, celebratory and human. It is an affirmation of earthly life and a healthy striving to approach the realm of the Gods. It deepens the link between humanity and the Divine, not with destruction and humiliation, but through joyous rituals, myth-creation, dance, music and communal celebrations, which link us to the wonderful spiritual world of our ancestors, instead of alienating us from it…" [4]

Why is scientific theory so widely accepted? Well, it's a commonly held belief that nothing exists outside of nature. Natural law exists at all levels of the Cosmos. With this being so, everything that exists or occurs, no matter how spectacular or incredible, happens because it is natural to do so despite whether or not we can comprehend it, or explain it at a particular time based on the current levels of technology or our own human limitations. Unlike Abrahamic faiths, man is not perceived as separate from their environment, or separate from the Universe. We were not created to be wards, stewards, or gardeners for "God's creation," and do not have dominion.

---

[4] Christianity has great moral messages, what does your religion offer? (2006) In *Supreme Council of Ethnikoi Hellenes*. Retrieved April 12, 2007, from http://www.ysee.gr/index-eng.php?type=english&f=faq#11

Ethics

THE ETHICAL CODE of Hellenismos is derived, by many, primarily from the Maxims of Delphi, but there are also the Tenets of Solon, the Ethics of Aristotle, the Golden Verses of Pythagoras, the philosophy of Epicurus and the Stoics. The one big difference between the Maxims and (as an example) the Ten Commandments used by Christians and Jews is the absence of the "shall not's." The Maxims are more focused on how one should behave rather than limiting or condemning individual personal behavior. Sometimes the differences on the surface may seem insignificant, but upon further examination they are often distinct.

Compare the commandment "You shall not commit murder" with the Delphic Maxim to "Shun murder." They seem to be saying the same thing but let's look deeper. The commandment "You shall not commit murder" is pretty straightforward in saying that you, personally, will not take the life of another person in cold blood. The Maxim to "Shun murder" says something slightly different. It says to reject all taking of a life in cold blood. The maxim instructs us to take an active role in insuring that murder is not committed, not just limiting us from committing it ourselves.

For me, there are three prime principles which are key to the ethics of Hellenismos. They are "Honor the Gods," "Give back what you have received," and "Nothing to excess."

"Honor the Gods" is a very important principal to focus on. We must ask ourselves how to do that, look at other maxims, and delve into the ancient texts. For the ancient Greeks and modern practitioners, honoring the Gods can be summed up with the word piety, the devout fulfillment of religious obligations.

Piety means simply to be devout, to show reverence to the Gods and to have an earnest wish to fulfill religious obligations. This ethic not only means participating in the public expressions of faith in ritual, but also acts of personal devotion: daily prayers and offerings, contemplation, pilgrimages, et al. Piety, for a practitioner of Hellenismos, literally means living your faith.

"Give back what you have received" can be described as the pinnacle of a group of maxims and ancient guidance that can be called inclusively the Laws of Reciprocity. These ethics define all relationships for a practitioner, including our relationship with the Gods. Many reading this may understand this as the principle "as you give, so shall you receive."

The Laws of Reciprocity is somewhat similar to "as you give, so shall you receive," but dictates as you receive, so shall you give. Children must respect their parents, but parents are expected to be worthy of that respect. Strangers are greeted and welcomed with overwhelming hospitality, and as a stranger one must be gracious of a host's generosity. One must remain loyal to friends and aid them as needed. Enemies are enemies until differences can be resolved. No one petitions the Gods empty handed, and the Gods do not turn their backs on their followers.

We also look to Hesiod, in Works and Days, who cites these reciprocal bonds needed to keep order as parent and child, host and guest, siblings, friends, and enemies. Neglecting appropriate reciprocal relationships is tempting misfortune. The Gods, themselves, will defend these associations as sacred.

"Nothing to excess" reinforces those virtues which describes the Hellenic ethic of moderation. Aristotle stated, "...since people desire honor both more and less than is right, it is also possible to desire it in the right way... When compared with love of honor, it appears as indifference to honor; when compared with indifference, it appears as love of honor; and when compared with both, it appears in a way as both. This would seem to be true with the other virtues too..." [5]

---

[5] Aristotle: The Nicomachean Ethics

Aristotle's prescription states to find virtue one must take an intermediate position between extremes.

This idea of moderation is again echoed in the wisdom of Plato, "Excess generally causes reaction, and produces a change in the opposite direction, whether it be in the seasons, or in individuals, or in governments." [6] The call for moderation is seen further and reinforced within the Maxims. "If you are a stranger act like one," "Control anger," "Exercise prudence," "Despise insolence," and "Act when you know" are just a few examples where the Maxims instruct us to act with moderation. But even moderation needs to be taken in moderation as Dionysus teaches us in his Mysteries.

As with any religion there is always a debate over what is and is not ethical behavior; thus what are and what are not appropriate political issues to support as a result. I wish to state this emphatically, Hellenic Polytheistic Reconstructionists are as diverse as they come. We are not of one mind on any issue. We are Republicans and Democrats, Conservatives and Liberals, Capitalists and Socialists. Beyond protecting religious rights and keeping Hellenic Polytheistic Reconstructionists safe from discrimination and defamation, there are no political activist issues that are globally defined as Hellenic. The notion that we, as a group, are united behind specific causes is not a factual statement and becomes an unproductive, dogmatic, one-sided argument.

It has been my experience that Hellenic Reconstructionists in America are divided up into the same so-called red and blue states just as the rest of the general population is. I have found that Hellenic Reconstructionists living in southern states tend to be very Conservative in their thinking and will lean toward issues of pro-life, will favor the death penalty, and support gun owners' rights. Hellenics living in the north-east and the west will, many times, be very pro-choice, will favor welfare programs, and will be environmental activists.

It all really begs the question, does religion influence our morals and ethics, or do the morals and ethics of our culture affect how we interpret the ethical codes provided by religion? Ultimately I believe each influences the other in addition to our own innate sense of right and

---

[6] Plato: Republic

wrong. Plato had said, "Good people do not need laws to tell them to act responsibly, while bad people will find a way around the laws." Let's be honest, who really needs to tell you that killing your neighbor, raping his wife, and taking his stuff is wrong?

Maxims of Delphi [7]

1. Follow the Divine
2. Obey the law
3. Honor the Gods
4. Respect your parents
5. Be overcome by justice
6. Know what you have learned
7. Perceive what you have heard
8. Be Yourself
9. Intend to get married
10. Know your opportunity
11. Think as a mortal
12. If you are a stranger act like one
13. Honor the hearth (or Hestia)
14. Control yourself
15. Help your friends
16. Control anger
17. Exercise prudence
18. Honor providence
19. Do not use an oath
20. Love friendship
21. Cling to discipline
22. Pursue honor
23. Long for wisdom
24. Praise the good
25. Find fault with no one
26. Praise virtue
27. Practice what is just
28. Be kind to friends
29. Watch out for your enemies
30. Exercise nobility of character
31. Shun evil
32. Be impartial
33. Guard what is yours
34. Shun what belongs to others
35. Listen to everyone

---

[7] The Commandments of the Seven (the copy of Sosiades preserved by Stobaeus)

36. Be (religiously) silent
37. Do a favor for a friend
38. Nothing to excess
39. Use time sparingly
40. Foresee the future
41. Despise insolence
42. Have respect for suppliants
43. Be accommodating in everything
44. Educate your sons
45. Give what you have
46. Fear deceit
47. Speak well of everyone
48. Be a seeker of wisdom
49. Choose what is divine
50. Act when you know
51. Shun murder
52. Pray for things possible
53. Consult the wise
54. Test the character
55. Give back what you have received
56. Down-look no one
57. Use your skill
58. Do what you mean to do
59. Honor a benefaction
60. Be jealous of no one
61. Be on your guard
62. Praise hope
63. Despise a slanderer
64. Gain possessions justly
65. Honor good men
66. Know the judge
67. Master wedding-feasts
68. Recognize fortune
69. Flee a pledge
70. Speak plainly
71. Associate with your peers
72. Govern your expenses
73. Be happy with what you have
74. Revere a sense of shame
75. Fulfill a favor
76. Pray for happiness

77. Be fond of fortune
78. Observe what you have heard
79. Work for what you can own
80. Despise strife
81. Detest disgrace
82. Restrain the tongue
83. Keep yourself from insolence
84. Make just judgments
85. Use what you have
86. Judge incorruptibly
87. Accuse one who is present
88. Tell when you know
89. Do not depend on strength
90. Live without sorrow
91. Live together meekly
92. Finish the race without shrinking back
93. Deal kindly with everyone
94. Do not curse your sons
95. Rule your wife
96. Benefit yourself
97. Be courteous
98. Give a timely response
99. Struggle with glory
100. Act without repenting
101. Repent of sins
102. Control the eye
103. Give a timely counsel
104. Act quickly
105. Guard friendship
106. Be grateful
107. Pursue harmony
108. Keep deeply the top secret
109. Fear ruling
110. Pursue what is profitable
111. Accept due measure
112. Do away with enmities
113. Accept old age
114. Do not boast in might
115. Exercise (religious) silence
116. Flee enmity
117. Acquire wealth justly

118. Do not abandon honor
119. Despise evil
120. Venture into danger prudently
121. Do not tire of learning
122. Do not stop to be thrifty
123. Admire oracles
124. Love whom you rear
125. Do not oppose someone absent
126. Respect the elder
127. Teach a youngster
128. Do not trust wealth
129. Respect yourself
130. Do not begin to be insolent
131. Crown your ancestors
132. Die for your country
133. Do not be discontented by life
134. Do not make fun of the dead
135. Share the load of the unfortunate
136. Gratify without harming
137. Grieve for no one
138. Beget rom noble routes
139. Make promises to no one
140. Do not wrong the dead
141. Be well off as a mortal
142. Do not trust fortune
143. As a child be well-behaved
144. As a youth - self-disciplined
145. As of middle-age - just
146. As an old man - sensible
147. On reaching the end - without sorrow

The only ethic that I truly believe is out of date is the one which states, "Rule your wife." I tend to think that "Rule your spouse" is more appropriate in modern times. The modern western world recognizes the fact that marriage is an equal partnership. It is the responsibility of each partner to be the others keeper, a check and balances viewpoint if you will.

Role of Clergy

IN MANY MAINSTREAM religions, the clergy are those individuals who are responsible for handling the ritual aspects of religious life, also taking the lead in spreading the doctrine of a particular religion. The role of clergy, within many religions, is as the spiritual leader of a congregation with broad powers and responsibilities which include teaching, counseling, and guidance. They often lead work for social change, awareness, and provide social services to the community. Clergy from many mainstream religions are distinguished as being the only ones authorized to perform rituals and, as a result, they act as intermediaries between believers and their God.

Hellenismos takes a decidedly different approach. The priests and priestesses in Hellenismos have a limited role in the religious life of practitioners, with many rituals (including weddings and funerals) being handled by the family. Anyone can approach the Gods; anyone can make offerings. The role of priests or priestesses is one, in most cases, of simply an office held by respected Elders elected by the community. Because the practice of Hellenismos is so heavily centered on personal devotion and family, there is little practical distinction between the religious authority of the priesthood and the laity.

This is not to say that priests and priestesses don't play a valuable role within a Hellenic Reconstructionist's practice. They absolutely do. Those working as clergy are going to be recognized Elders within the community. In the modern practice, and as a result of limited numbers of practitioners, those performing the role of clergy are also those who have taken a lead role by either founding religious organizations, acting as scholars, or in generally promoting a positive image of Hellenismos.

Duties of clergy include presiding over public rituals, organizing and taking part in festivals, being caretakers of sacred sites, and handling the day to day business affairs of a temple, cult, or religious organization.

Religious practice within Hellenismos is broken down into layers. There is the public practice which includes public rituals and festivals, cult practice which focuses on the mysteries of individual Gods and Goddesses, and there are the personal devotional practices. It can also be said that, within Hellenismos, all religion is local; as a result, practices are not universal. If a temple is created to honor Athena in Philadelphia, it is not expected to mirror the practices of a temple dedicated to Athena in Los Angeles. The duties assigned to a priest or priestess will be different from place to place, temple to temple, and cult to cult.

How a person receives the title and office of priest or priestess will even differ depending on the particular location, organization, or individual temple. Mimicking the practices of ancient Greece, clergy may be placed in the office through a number of different methods. Some of those methods could include election or lottery from a list of nominated individuals.

One method that could be employed, but is generally not heard of at this time, is becoming a priest or priestess through inheritance or by bequest. This method was used in some cases in ancient times and could be employed today by those individuals who, on their own, erect temples or create religious organizations that are self owned. In these cases, the role of temple priest or priestess could be passed down to one's descendants either at a desired time or willed as part of an estate.

The purchase of a priesthood was also employed in ancient Greece and is a method that can be adapted for a modern practice. I have not actually heard of this method being used by any modern practitioners, and I believe many may find the technique distasteful, but it could be applied in a form which some could see as palatable. One idea could be that the highest contributing member of a temple receives the right to act as priest for a limited time, similar to an individual who becomes a priest through a right of ownership. Another suggestion could be that person who is the most effective fundraiser.

Historians grant the title of priest to many roles in ancient Greece, from the actual temple priests and priestesses to prophets and oracles to ritual torch bearers and temple sweepers. I believe there is great benefit to taking this tack when dealing with modern clergy. There are many roles that can be performed within the religion we can universally classify as clergy, each with a specific title based on their role either as officiant, scholar, teacher, or simply ritual participant.

It can be said that the person best to "lead" a religious organization (be it temple, cult, or other structure) is not necessarily the best person to lead ritual. The best person to lead rituals is not necessarily the best person to be in the role of head theologian or scholar. The best scholar is not necessarily the best person in the role as teacher. The best teacher is not necessarily the best person to be in the role of counselor. I think you get the idea. Having one person with ultimate authority within a group or congregation, even if those other roles are delegated, that group or congregation can then find themselves limited by the sensibilities of the individual leader and the sensibilities of those that person then reports to in the chain of command.

The legal ordination of clergy is also of great importance in our modern practice of Hellenismos. With a few exceptions based on the practices of individual cults, there was no official ordination process in ancient times that granted individuals the right to perform ceremonies and rituals as we would define it today. In fact, it was just assumed that anyone could petition the Gods or perform sacrifices. It was also a matter of fact that families could and did perform their own rites of passage, including weddings and funerals. The only purpose I find in needing ordination (specifically in the United States but I'm sure it's valid in many other parts of the world) is to conform to any state or local laws regarding the officiating of certain ceremonies.

A positive note is that not all states in the Union actually require ordination to perform legal ceremonies such as weddings. The state of California, for example, at the time this book was written, allows individuals the right to purchase a one day permit granting virtually anyone the ability to officiate a wedding. The Commonwealth of Pennsylvania, the first British colony in the Americas to legally embrace freedom of religion for all its citizens, has very liberal laws when it comes to officiating. The Pennsylvania law is written in such a way that any person from within a religious organization can marry a couple as long as at least one person is a part of that organization and it is a traditional practice. Pennsylvania also grants couples the option of obtaining a

"Quaker marriage license," effectively allowing couples to marry themselves without clergy.

Some states and localities are not so lucky. I know from a personal experience that the City of New York has some restrictions that could make officiating legal ceremonies difficult. In New York City even legally ordained clergy in good standing are not granted the right to perform marriages unless that clergy is a part of an actual religious organization which has a local congregation that meets the city's definition. There are even some states that include very restrictive wording on who is authorized to perform these services. They will use phrases such as "minister of the gospel" and "rabbi" to effectively limit these rights to those within Abrahamic religions, and may cause issues for those attempting to perform these rites that would otherwise be qualified.

There are a number of different organizations granting legal ordination to practitioners of Hellenismos. Some organizations provide ordination on request with no limitations on who receives these credentials. These organizations are not necessarily Hellenic Reconstructionist in nature, like the Universal Life Church, but espouse a belief that all individuals have a right to worship as they choose. Other organizations have a limited educational process to insure that the petitioner for ordination credentials have at least a limited knowledge of the ancient Greek religion and are in fact Reconstructionist in their methods. Also, you will find that there are a few groups that are mimicking the strict hierarchal structures and rigid dogmatism of some mainstream churches.

I recommend those wishing to practice Hellenismos to seek out their ordination credentials (if needed or desired) from an organization that provides them on request, and I encourage more Hellenic Reconstructionist organizations to use this method. The ancient Greek religion was very family centered. Families intrinsically had the right to perform welcomings, weddings, funerals, and other rituals without having to go through intermediaries. Providing ordination credentials on request returns these rights back to individuals and their families as they should be.

One should also expect that if a priest or priestess is employed in any fashion, they should be paid for their services in some way, shape, or form. In ancient times, priests and priestesses where entitled to a portion of the meat from the animal sacrifice which accompanied virtually every event. In the modern world it is unlikely practitioners will be performing regular animal sacrifices, and sending an officiant off with a fifty-pound slab of beef is simply not practical. Some may see paying for ritual services the same as "paying" for the right to practice their religion, but this is not so. Individuals who take the time to perform these rites and rituals are providing a valuable service to our community; they deserve some form of gratuity. Priests and priestesses in ancient times were compensated for their time and effort, and so should they today.

Rituals & Rites of Passage

THE RITUALS AND rites of Hellenismos, like most religious rites, are ceremonious acts that very often fall within one of three classifications: rites of passage, rites of worship, and rites of personal devotion. Rites of passage are ceremonies which mark the changing of an individual's social status, such as weddings or funerals. A rite of worship is when a community comes together for worship, such as public rituals or festivals. Rites of personal devotion are where an individual worships alone or within the family, this includes prayer and meditation.

Within modern Hellenismos, as in ancient times, all religion is local and most times include the addition of personalized family centered traditions. It becomes at some point an impossible task to do justice to the many practices that are out there. Each of the individual groups, despite basing their practice on some of the same source material, will tend to do things in their own special way. The rites performed are, in many respects, similar in premise to rites which you may already be familiar from mainstream churches.

Welcoming and Naming Ceremonies are common terms used for a rite that is very similar in context to a Christening or Baptism in some Christian faiths. These ceremonies mark the arrival of a new life into the world. The child, on the day they are brought home from the hospital, is presented to the hearth (Hestia), asked to be protected by the Agathosdaemon, and is granted a name. In some forms of the rite a pledge is made by the parents, "God-parents," and (sometimes) the local tradition's membership to be responsible for the spiritual welfare of the new child; also vowing to keep them safe until adulthood.

There are many things a family can include in a "coming of age rite," considered similar in general context to a Catholic Confirmation, Jewish Bat mitzvah and Bar mitzvah, and the Baptism in some Christian faiths. Within these rites and rituals a child would be identified as walking thru the doorway from childhood into spiritual adulthood, taking the responsibility of their own spirituality on themselves. I truly believe these should be grand events including a sacrifice, a large feast, athletic events, and poetry contests. One can really let their imagination run with such a family centered experience. I also emphatically recommend that no matter what is done, the child should perform an act (they prepared) leaving them with a sense of accomplishment, that they earned the right to be called an adult.

Other rites of passage may include initiations, weddings, menopause, and death.

Rites of worship are the regular meetings for worship by a group, and again tend to be customized to the specific local Hellenic Reconstructionists while still being very much based on the public rituals and festivals of ancient Greece. Local practitioners of Hellenismos may have their own rites of worship based on the records of the religious practice of a specific city-state, and may have created some unique locally recognized rituals and festivals as well. We will go into greater detail about this in the next chapter, but even though Hellenismos is an attempt to recreate, the practice encourages innovation, localization, and personalization within an ancient Greek context.

Rites of personal devotion are how an individual worships on a day to day basis and may include sacrifices, prayer, meditation, pilgrimages, or other acts. Rites of personal devotion are just that, personal, but can be very formal or informal depending on the individual themselves. These acts could include morning and evening prayers, daily meditation, offerings, fasting, and any number of acts one may perform to honor the Gods, Goddesses, ancestors, or other divinities.

Personal devotion is at the very heart of modern Hellenismos. It would not be unheard of to have an outdoor altar (outdoor fireplaces work well for this) for sacrifices, a shrine or shrines dedicated to the worship of specific Gods and Goddesses, or a lamp to house the sacred flame of Hestia. The burning of incense or lighting of candles is often common offerings, in addition to the giving of libations and portions of daily meals. All this is done because of reciprocity and the knowledge that the Gods honor these laws. Practitioners of Hellenismos work in creating a personal relationship with their Gods, their ancestors, and other (including local) divinities. Because these relationships are known to be reciprocal, one does not approach the Gods empty handed. Even though there is nothing that we can give the Gods that they can't obtain themselves, the act of sharing what one has is an important symbol of devotion.

Prayers in Hellenic worship follow a formula and can be partitioned into three segments. All prayers begin with an invocation or calling of the God or Goddess. During this opening the petitioner invites the deity to listen and will reference many of their epithets, feats, and governances. The second section of the prayer one states the reason why the God or Goddess should hear the prayer, citing the supplicant's devotion and listing what they have done for the deity in the past. Prayers then end with the petitioner's request.

A short and simple prayer example:

Queen Aphrodite, who is the Fairest, Laughter Loving, and Heavenly;
I have made offerings to you of emeralds, turquoise, and roses;
Please help my partner remember why she fell in love with me.

The basic ritual structure is relatively straightforward and typically performed outdoors. One should open with a procession where all the participants enter the sacred place and approach an altar. The altar can be a permanent structure or one set up temporarily prior to beginning the ritual. All the ritual tools and offerings are then set up appropriately; participants take their spots.

Purification is the next step. The acting priest or priestess will ritually cleanse themselves using a mixture of pure water and sea salt, sprinkling the water then over the altar and any offerings. The initial offering is of barley. The priest will speak a prayer, hymn, or other calling followed by the participants throwing handfuls of barley onto the altar.

The next step is in preparation to the primary offering. The priest or priestess will take a snippet of the offering throwing it into a fire, a bit of hair or some such inconsequential piece. The primary sacrifice is then slaughtered, broken, torn or spilled out. The sacrificed item(s) are then segmented. The first share of the sacrifice will be offered to Hestia, followed by a share of the offering being set aside for the Gods. This portion will be burned or placed in a pit in the earth depending on whether it is intended for the Olympians or the Chthonian. Offerings are then made to the deity associated with the festival. Offerings of wine, milk or other liquids are then poured on the fire and a portion of drinkable items will be placed in a bowl or chalice for participants to sip from, the remains poured on the floor or ground.

At the conclusion of the ritual the consumable offerings are cooked and shared. These items should be eaten at the ritual site with some portion made available for the officiating priest or priestess to take home with them.

When performing rituals, special care needs to be taken when choosing a sacred place. The area can be either rural or urban but must be recognized as having divine power. It is not necessary that the land be sectioned off or have a building; one should look for natural features such as a cave, natural spring, or a grove. Organizations that don't have access to the sacred sites in Greece may want to consider purchasing land they have identified as sacred to erect modern temples.

I'll end this section with a discussion on offerings. Generally, offerings take two forms: sacrifices and votives. Sacrifices are typically offerings made of consumable items and are burned. Votive offerings are gifts to the Gods or offerings made as part of fulfilling a vow. The purpose of offerings is as a token gift in gratitude to the Gods, ensuring their continued attention. The practice is very closely associated with the Laws of Reciprocity we discussed earlier, which the Gods are believed to honor and uphold.

The first thing typically coming to one's mind when discussing sacrifices is an animal sacrifice. I will by no means tell you not to perform one, but I will suggest that if you attempt to perform an animal sacrifice that you take the time to do thorough research. It must be done properly. Most modern practitioners refrain from performing animal sacrifices. Some believing that the act is not necessary, others citing man's disconnect from the natural world.

> "...letting of blood... is not easily appreciated, because
> humanity has distanced itself from nature and consumes

meat slaughtered savagely with mechanical devices, bought in supermarkets and packaged in plastic. This is why we only persist with the practice of blood-less sacrifice." [8]

While most practitioners do not push the issue, religious sacrifice is legal in the US and was upheld by the US Supreme Court in 1993 with the case "Church of Lukumi Babalu Aye v. City of Hialeah" (508 U.S. 520).

The Church of Lukumi Babalu Aye is a Santeria Church practicing animal sacrifice. The city of Hialeah, after finding out about the church's practices, passed a law banning animal sacrifice on the grounds that it was "unnecessary," a community health risk, and cruel to the animals. The court found that the law unjustly targeted religious expression; the law was overturned.

Many animal rights activists may take issue with animal sacrifice, claiming that it is cruel. If one follows proper ritual procedures the killings are conducted in a safe and humane manner. The priests charged with doing the sacrifice should be trained in humane ways to kill the animals. Additionally, the animals must always be cooked and eaten afterwards.

Libations are another form of sacrifice, and are much more common and easier to perform. A libation is an offering of wine, milk, oil, or other such liquid item which are poured on the floor, altar, or ground. This sacrifice can be made by giving the first portion after opening a container or at the beginning of meals. Libations are also included as part of most rituals.

Votive offerings or votive deposits are gifts, left at sacred places, to the Gods or other divinities. These offerings can take many shapes including the giving of artwork, poetry, jewelry, or any of an unlimited list of items which may have meaning to you or a symbolic connection to the deity. Incense, herbs, or flowers can also be given as offerings; burning them is considered a modest sacrifice and can be included in daily personal devotions.

---

[8] Do you perform blood sacrifices? (2006) In *Supreme Council of Ethnikoi Hellenes.* Retrieved April 12, 2007, from http://www.ysee.gr/index-eng.php?type=english&f=faq#36

Once a votive offering has been made the item is the property of the divinity it was offered to. You can no longer receive a personal benefit from its use. Items which may be left out in nature tend not to be an issue, but other items which are kept on behalf of a divinity may cause temptation. Some practitioners keep a "vault" that allow offerings to be kept either indefinitely, until used, or until donated to charity. The treatment of these items is very important. If you offer jewelry you can't then pull it out when you go to the boss' retirement party. In my opinion, the profits from a book written as an offering to the Gods are not yours. You may not use charitable contributions made on behalf of a deity as a write-off on your taxes. One must be sure that all offerings made are done so with all due piety and without hubris.

Holidays & Festivals

HELLENIC RECONSTRUCTIONISTS VERY often use a lunar festival calendar which encompasses 12 to 13 months, depending on the specific year. I will be using for this discussion a calendar based primarily on that of ancient Athens. Their calendar begins with the first new moon after the Summer Solstice and consists of 12-13 months of 29-30 days. There are three weeks in each month broken into 9-10 days each. Days begin and end at dusk and are segmented into 12 daylight hours and 12 nighttime hours. These hours vary in actual length but the result is that noon is literally midday and midnight is literally the middle of the night. This Hellenic religious calendar will then consist of both monthly observances to different divinities and more then sixty annual festivals, some lasting for several days.

Remember, these calendars will be localized and each temple, cult, or organization may include modern festivals in addition to ancient ones. Also, the new moon does not occur at the same time in Athens, Greece as it does in (let's say) Philadelphia, Pennsylvania, and as a result religious celebrations may occur on different actual days of the civil calendar. The idea that one should honor local spirits is also an idea that is often embraced by many. This results in many Hellenic Reconstructionists in North America, Australia, and other areas honoring the local divinities of the First Nation peoples in addition to the Greek Gods.

The months of a Hellenic festival calendar include:

1. Hekatombaion (July)
2. Metageitnion (August)
3. Boedromion (September)

4. Puanepsion (October)
5. Maimakterion (November)
6. Poseideon (December)
7. Poseideon II – An interposed month placed after Poseideon in "leap years."
8. Gamelion (January)
9. Anthesterion (February)
10. Elaphebolion (March)
11. Mounukhion (April)
12. Thargelion (May)
13. Skirophorion (June)

The monthly observances for Hellenic Reconstructionists will start on the new moon and include:

1. 1st of the month: *Noumenia* - new moon festival
2. 2nd of the month – Agathosdaemon
3. 3rd of the month - Athena
4. 4th of the month - Aphrodite, Hermes, Heracles, Eros
5. 6th of the month - Artemis
6. 7th of the month - Apollo
7. 8th of the month - Poseidon
8. last day - *Hena Kai Nea*, the 'old and the new', Hecate

There are many, many annual festivals. These various celebrations have a range of popularity and importance among practitioners of Hellenismos, as they also did in ancient Greece. Each festival will be uniquely designed around the divinity being honored, having their own events and unique rituals, but will include a few common elements that we touched on in the previous chapter. Included will be a procession to a shrine, temple, or other sacred space. There is typically the decorating or dressing of a statue of the deity or other symbolic images. Sacrifices will occur and there will be proceedings that include the singing of hymns, athletic events and contests of music, drama, and poetry.

In researching some of these events you may find that there are festivals which are so closely tied with the original location it may be difficult to reconstruct them locally. Some of these festivals may even seem inappropriate to reproduce outside the original setting. Do not fret. Local adaptation and innovation is part and parcel to Hellenismos. There is nothing inherently wrong with making adaptations to festivals or to completely omit them if doing so seems to be the most pious course of action.

Hekatombaion, Month of

12th – Kronia: Festival to honor Cronus.
16th – Synoecia: Annual sacrifice celebrating the people of Attica.
23rd-30th – Panathenaea: This festival climaxes on the 28th and is in celebration of Athena's birth.

Metageitnion, Month of

15th-18th – Eleusinia: This is a four day celebration of games held every four years on the second year of the Olympiad.
16th – Sacrifice to Kourotrophos, Hecate, and Artemis.
19th – Sacrifice to "the Heroines."
20th – Sacrifice to Hera Thelchinia.
25th – Sacrifice to Zeus Epoptes.

Boedromion, Month of

4th – Sacrifice to Basile.
5th – Genesia: Festival of the Dead.
6th – Sacrifice to Artemis Agrotera.
12th – Democratia: Festival to honor democracy.
15th-21st – Eleusinian Mysteries: (also the Great Mysteries) Rites celebrating Persephone and Demeter.
17th – Epidauria: Festival to honor Asclepius.
27th – Sacrifices to the Nymphs, Achelous, Hermes, Athena, and Gaia.

Puanepsion, Month of

6th – Proerosia: A first fruits agricultural festival.
7th – Puanepsia: Festival in honor of Apollo.
8th – Theseia: Festival in honor of Theseus.
8th – Oschophoria: A grape harvest festival.
9th – Stenia: A women's festival in honor of Demeter and Persephone.
11th-13th – Thesmophoria: A women's festival in honor of Demeter.

14th – Sacrifice to "the Heroines."

19th-21st – Apaturia: A celebration of the phratries which include rites of passage.

30th – Chalceia: Festival to honor Athena and Hephaestus.

Maimakterion, Month of

Last week – Pompaia: Festival honoring Zeus Meilikhos.

Poseideon, Month of

16th – Sacrifice to Zues Horios.

Second half of month – Rural Dionysia: (or Rustic Dionysia) Festival honoring Dionysus.

26th – Haloa: Fertility festival for Dionysus and Demeter.

Gamelion, Month of

8th – Sacrifice to Apollo Apotropaeus, Apollo Nymphegetes, and the Nymphs.

9th – Sacrifice to Athena

12th-16th – Lenea: Festival to honor Dionysus.

27th – Theogamia: Celebration honoring the marriage of Hera and Zeus. Also sacrifices to Kourotrophos, Hera, Zeus Teleius, and Poseidon.

Anthesterion, Month of

2nd – Sacrifice to Dionysus.

11th-13th – Anthesteria: Festival honoring Dionysus.

20th-26th – Lesser Mysteries: Held in preparation for the Eleusinian Mysteries.

23rd – Diasia: Festival honoring Zeus Meilichios.

Elaphebolion, Month of

10th-17th – City Dionysia: (or Great Dionysia) Festival in honor of Dionysus.

15th – Sacrifice to Cronus.

17th – Pandia: Festival to honor Zeus.

Mounukhion, Month of

16th – Munichia: Festival to honor Artemis.
19th – Olympieia: Festival held for Olympian Zeus.
20th – Sacrifice to Leucaspis.
21st – Sacrifice to Tritopatores.

Thargelion, Month of

4th – Sacrifices to Leto, Pythian Apollo, Zeus, Hermes, and the Dioscuri.
7th – Thargelia: Festival to honor Apollo.
19th – Festival to honor the Thracian Goddess Bendis.
25th – Plynteria: Festival (of Washing) honoring Athena.

Skirophorion, Month of

3rd – Arrephoria: Festival honoring Athena.
3rd – Sacrifices to Kourotrophos, Athena Polias, Aglaurus, Zeus Polieus, Poseidon, and Pandrosus.
12th – Scira: A woman focused festival honoring Demeter.
14th – Bouphonia: Festival honoring Zeus Polieus.

There are a number of festivals that I omitted from our list; the original dates were either unknown or undefined. One example of this is the Mysteries of Dionysus which had no specific cult site and seemed to be performed almost spontaneously wherever members gathered. It is up to you, when creating a local calendar, whether to incorporate these festivals and when such events are to be practiced, if at all.

Divination

DIVINATION IS THE practice, in a religious sense, of obtaining knowledge through communication with divine sources and through the reading of omens, oracles, signs and portents; sometimes referred to as prophecy. The belief is that the Gods are communicating their will, guiding people to take the appropriate path or to make right choices. Divination appears to occur in virtually all the world's religions in one form or another, not just in ancient Greece.

Many forms of divination exist, but some Hellenic Reconstructionists may have limitations on what forms are appropriate for themselves or even for others. While I'll refrain from making specific examples here to avoid controversy, there are those who find certain divinatory practices so closely tied to the religion that offense is taken when others attempt them.

Some common forms of divination include:

> **Aeromancy** - divination conducted by interpreting atmospheric conditions.
>
> **Astrology** - several systems in which knowledge of the positions of celestial bodies is held to be useful in understanding, interpreting, and organizing knowledge.
>
> **Biorhythms divination** - uses the hypothetical cyclic pattern of alterations in physiology, emotions, and/or intellect.
>
> **Cartomancy** - divination using cards, including playing cards, tarot cards, and non-tarot oracle cards.

Chaomancy - the interpreting of atmospheric conditions.

Dice divination - conducted by interpreting the roll of dice.

Graphology - the interpreting of handwriting in connection to behavior, personal information and other traits.

Lampadomancy - a form of divination using a single oil lamp or a torch flame.

Libanomancy - the use of books, typically sacred books, for divination. The Bible code is one example.

Metagnomy - divining using "visions" received in a trance state.

Necromancy - divination through the summoning of and communication with spirits.

Numerology -uses of esoteric numeric associations and interruptive meanings as a form of divination.

Oinomancy - uses of patterns created by wine as a form of divination, and is usually associated with priests and priestesses of Dionysus or Bacchus.

Ouija board divination - uses a Ouija board, talking board, or spirit board to communicate with spirits.

Palmistry - the divinatory reading of the hands.

Ornithomancy - the Ancient Greek practice of oracle reading the behavior of birds.

Zoomancy - the divinatory interpretation of the appearance and behavior of animals.

We can separate divination into two categories: artificial and natural. Artificial divination is the interpretation of external phenomenon or devices. Natural divination includes the interpretation of dreams, visions, or other forms of direct communication from the Gods, spirits, or other entities.

Artificial divination covers a large spectrum of methods. The observation of birds and animals, the interpreting of their behaviors as signs or omens is one method. Astrology, by studying the movement of the stars, planets, and other celestial bodies, assigning them meaning, is also a form of artificial divination. Other forms of artificial divination include Tarot, reading animal entrails, tea leaves or the reading of wine stains on cloth.

Natural divination is defined as such because the communication, in one form or another, is being transmitted through you or another person. The interpretation of dreams is considered a natural method, as well as chance remarks within a conversation. Forms of divination which are a direct communication with the dead are considered to be natural. These methods can also come to be seen under the title of prophecy, because it is believed that the Gods are speaking through the individual.

The most famous form of natural divination, from ancient Greece, is the oracle. An oracle is a person who is through direct communication with a deity, an oracle is also considered to be able to predict the future. Ancient Greece had many sites dedicated to dispensing of oracular wisdom; the most notable is the priestess of Apollo at Delphi.

Oracles are priests or priestesses who, when entering an altered state of consciousness, receive messages from their respective God or Goddess. They are acting as an agent or medium, thus are considered to be in direct communion with the deity. There were various methods employed by many ancient oracles to induce the states required to communicate with a God or Goddess, they include the chewing of toxic herbs or inhaling poisonous vapors.

Magic vs. Mystical

SOME, TYPICALLY AMERICAN, practitioners of Hellenismos embrace and incorporate the practice of magic(k). I believe we need to look very closely at the terms, Magic and Mysticism, because they are not interchangeable though both require the belief in the "supernatural." Magic is any act of employing one's own will, desire, and intent to cause deliberate change. Mysticism is the practice of direct communion with a God, Goddess, divinity, or ultimate reality.

The standard line one hears regarding the practice of magic and Hellenismos is that "magic exists outside the religion." It is believed that magic did exist in ancient Greece, though some evidence suggests no "magicians" were present in Classical Greece or later. Magic was not, in any case, a part of any mainstream practices. Some practitioners of modern Hellenismos interpret history to mean that magic and spellcraft may be practiced as long as it is segregated from all Hellenic worship. I tend to disagree. The ancient Greeks did not separate the spiritual world from the secular. While city-states would not necessarily meet today's definition of theocracies, spiritual practices existed at all levels, intertwined with both public and private life. Spirituality was so a matter of fact that the ancient Greeks did not even have a word for religion.

Magic today has come to be used as a catchall. One needs to initially separate out shamanistic, mystical, and divination practices of the ancient Greeks because, to them, this was not magic. Most of the forms of magic remaining, like spellcraft, would then either violate Hellenic ethical and moral sensibilities or are forms that would be considered impious and/or hubris. Any form of magic performed where the practitioner believes that they are wielding power in and of themselves would be hubris. Any form of magick where the practitioner believes that they are commanding or are in control of the Gods will be seen as impious.

Shamanistic practices are those that ask spirits and divine beings to aid and guide you in your work. Mysticism is a ritual or other practice that creates a direct connection with deity. Divination, in the religious sense, is a form of communication. If a person wants to call these things "magick" that's fine I guess, but outside of those, where one is supposedly wielding power or in control, it will be considered hubris and can often be impious.

Many modern Neopagans and Wiccans look at a priestess like that at Delphi, the Oracle, and will identify her as a witch. She was no such thing. She was the elected priestess of Apollo who was used by the Gods as a vessel, conduit, and medium to convey information to mortals. She claimed no power of herself as what she performed was an act of devotion and piety towards the Gods.

Magic, at its core, is about manipulation and directly attempting to make something happen. Whether it's to heal or hurt, bind or repel, create or destroy, magic is a process by which the manipulation of either the spiritual or mundane world occurs. For the uneducated, they may see no difference in the magic performed by some of today's Neopagans and Wiccans with the rituals of Hellenismos, but surface appearances can be deceiving.

Let's compare a basic spell with a method of petitioning the Gods used in Hellenismos. A Neopagan or Wiccan may write their spell on a piece of parchment, read it aloud, and then cast it into a fire along with a "magical" blend of incense to boost the effectiveness. A practitioner of Hellenismos may write a prayer on a piece of parchment, read it aloud, and then cast it into a fire along with an offering of incense.

The Neopagan or Wiccan believes that the power comes from them creating the spell, reading it, casting its energy into the universe by burning it, and that the spell gets a little boost by burning a bit of incense specially formulated for magical purposes. The practitioner of Hellenismos is petitioning the Gods for their assistance by creating, reading, and burning the prayer. The offering is a gift in appreciation and anticipation of that assistance. The Neopagan or Wiccan believes it is their own energy that is creating change. The practitioner of Hellenismos knows that any change that may occur is by the will of the Gods alone.

Amulets give us another example to compare. Hermes is "Luck Bringing" and an aid to gamblers. Neopagans and Hellenics alike may wear an amulet bearing either his image or symbols if they are on a trip to Las Vegas or Atlantic City. The Neopagan sees the symbolism in the charm as having power in and of itself or in having the power to compel Hermes to assist them at the gambling table. The Hellenic Reconstructionist sees no power in the amulet itself and the idea that wearing it could force a God to aid one is impious. The wearing of the amulet is a devotional act, and an acknowledgment of Hermes' governances. It is hoped that by wearing it Hermes will grant his assistance, and the person most likely will complete offerings or make vows if the individual is truly seeking aid.

Mysticism, in comparison to magic, is a combination of practices that are understood to cause a direct spiritual union with a God, Goddess, divinity, or ultimate reality. There are many acts that can be used to stimulate mystical experiences such as dreams, words, phrases, music, art, sounds, smells, daydreaming, the play of light upon land and sea, nature, or a near-death experience. There are also specific acts that can be performed to self-induce an occurrence such as hypnosis, autohypnosis, flotation tanks, sensory deprivation, sleep deprivation, fasting, chanting, dancing, breath control, sexual rites, yoga, and meditation.

Mystical experience can manifest either internally or externally, and can provide an individual with a great wealth of personal gnosis. While mysticism does not have the same negative connotation placed on it by some groups as magic does, it still is not globally accepted or practiced among Hellenic Reconstructionists.

One example of mystical practice easily cited from ancient times is the practice of being an oracle. Oracles are priests or priestesses who, when entering an altered state of consciousness, receive messages from their respective God or Goddess. They are acting as an agent or medium, and thus are considered to be in spiritual union with the deity. The methods employed by many ancient oracles included the chewing of toxic herbs or inhaling poisonous vapors, so I do not recommend individuals attempt to recreate this practice at all.

The Mysteries of Dionysus are also viewed as mystical practice. These rites, called the *orgia*, are defined as ecstatic rituals. In today's world, most rituals are very controlled, but ecstatic rituals employ several methods including drumming, dancing, and consuming alcohol to alter one's state of consciousness; allowing for direct communion with deity. Other techniques of entering an ecstatic state include controlled breathing, sweating, fasting, and even consuming large amounts of caffeine. Under ecstatic states the participants are under divine influence and can experience dramatic changes in physiological responses and perceptions, visions, hallucinations, heightened intuition, and euphoria. It is believed that during the *orgia* that the Maenads, female worshipers of Dionysus, would sing and dance in the forest and on hilltops. The Maenads are said to have worked up such an ecstatic frenzy during their rites, they could pull trees from the ground and rip animals apart with their bare hands devouring the raw flesh.

My Neopagan friends will sometimes become concerned that I am judging or looking down on them for their practice of magic or spellcraft. Judging their behavior, I believe, is hubris. I explain my position to them this way, "The Gods are very often more accommodating to us then we are of them, but having said that they hold us to the paradigm that we are in. If you are within a structure that believes the three fold law, they are going to darn well give it to you. If you are within a system that comes to the conclusion that certain acts are impious, you will be held to that standard. The catch is that you can't just opt-out. One believes what they believe because they believe it, not because they don't want to be held accountable for their actions. If you believe like a Hellenic Reconstructionist but act like a Wiccan, you will be smacked down for it."

Appendix I:
Works And Days by Hesiod
translated by Hugh G. Evelyn-White (1914)
edited by Timothy Jay Alexander

(ll. 1-10) Muses of Pieria, who give glory through song, come hither, tell of Zeus your father and chant his praise. Through him mortal men are famed or un-famed, sung or unsung alike, as great Zeus wills. For easily he makes strong, and easily he brings the strong man low; easily he humbles the proud and raises the obscure, and easily he straightens the crooked and blasts the proud, -- Zeus who thunders aloft and has his dwelling most high.

Attend thou with eye and ear, and make judgments straight with righteousness. And I, Perses, would tell of true things.

(ll. 11-24) So, after all, there was not one kind of Strife alone, but all over the earth there are two. As for the one, a man would praise her when he came to understand her; but the other is blameworthy: and they are wholly different in nature. For one fosters evil war and battle, being cruel: her no man loves; but perforce, through the will of the deathless Gods, men pay harsh Strife her honor due. But the other is the elder daughter of dark Night, and the son of Cronos who sits above and dwells in the ether, set her in the roots of the earth: and she is far kinder to men. She stirs up even the shiftless to toil; for a man grows eager to work when he considers his neighbor, a rich man who hastens to plow and plant and put his house in good order; and neighbor vies with is neighbor as he hurries after wealth. This Strife is wholesome for men. And potter is angry with potter, and craftsman with craftsman, and beggar is jealous of beggar, and minstrel of minstrel.

(ll. 25-41) Perses, lay up these things in your heart, and do not let that Strife who delights in mischief hold your heart back from work, while you peep and peer and listen to the wrangles of the court-house. Little concern has he with quarrels and courts who has not a year's victuals laid up betimes, even that which the earth bears, Demeter's grain. When you have got plenty of that, you can raise disputes and strive to get another's goods. But you shall have no second chance to deal so again: nay, let us settle our dispute here with true judgment divided our inheritance, but you seized the greater share and carried it off, greatly swelling the glory of our bribe-swallowing lords who love to judge such a cause as this. Fools! They know not how much more the half is than the whole, nor what great advantage there is in mallow and asphodel (1).

(ll. 42-53) For the Gods keep hidden from men the means of life. Else you would easily do work enough in a day to supply you for a full year even without working; soon would you put away your rudder over the smoke, and the fields worked by ox and sturdy mule would run to waste. But Zeus in the anger of his heart hid it, because Prometheus the crafty deceived him; therefore he planned sorrow and mischief against men. He hid fire; but that the noble son of Iapetus stole again for men from Zeus the counselor in a hollow fennel-stalk, so that Zeus who delights in thunder did not see it. But afterwards Zeus who gathers the clouds said to him in anger:

(ll. 54-59) 'Son of Iapetus, surpassing all in cunning, you are glad that you have outwitted me and stolen fire -- a great plague to you yourself and to men that shall be. But I will give men as the price for fire an evil thing in which they may all be glad of heart while they embrace their own destruction.'

(ll. 60-68) So said the father of men and Gods, and laughed aloud. And he bade famous Hephaestus make haste and mix earth with water and to put in it the voice and strength of human kind, and fashion a sweet, lovely maiden-shape, like to the immortal Goddesses in face; and Athena to teach her needlework and the weaving of the varied web; and golden Aphrodite to shed grace upon her head and cruel longing and cares that weary the limbs. And he charged Hermes the guide, the Slayer of Argus, to put in her a shameless mind and a deceitful nature.

(ll. 69-82) So he ordered. And they obeyed the lord Zeus the son of Cronos. Forthwith the famous Lame God molded clay in the likeness of a modest maid, as the son of Cronos purposed. And the Goddess bright-eyed Athena girded and clothed her and the divine Graces and queenly Persuasion put necklaces of gold upon her, and the rich-haired Hours crowned her head with spring flowers. And Pallas Athena bedecked her form with all manners of finery. Also the Guide, the Slayer of Argus, contrived within her lies and crafty words and a deceitful nature at the will of loud thundering Zeus, and the Herald of the Gods put speech in her. And he called this woman Pandora (2), because all they who dwelt on Olympus gave each a gift, a plague to men who eat bread.

(ll. 83-89) But when he had finished the sheer, hopeless snare, the Father sent glorious Argus-Slayer, the swift messenger of the Gods, to take it to Epimetheus as a gift. And Epimetheus did not think on what Prometheus had said to him, bidding him never take a gift of Olympian Zeus, but to send it back for fear it might prove to be something harmful to men. But he took the gift, and afterwards, when the evil thing was already his, he understood.

(ll. 90-105) For ere this the tribes of men lived on earth remote and free from ills and hard toil and heavy sickness which bring the Fates upon men; for in misery men grow old quickly. But the woman took off the great lid of the jar (3) with her hands and scattered all these and her thought caused sorrow and mischief to men. Only Hope remained there in an unbreakable home within under the rim of the great jar, and did not fly out at the door; for ere that, the lid of the jar stopped her, by the will of Aegis-holding Zeus who gathers the clouds. But the rest, countless plagues, wander amongst men; for earth is full of evils and the sea is full. Of themselves diseases come upon men continually by day and by night, bringing mischief to mortals silently; for wise Zeus took away speech from them. So is there no way to escape the will of Zeus.

(ll. 106-108) Or if you will, I will sum you up another tale well and skillfully -- and do you lay it up in your heart, -- how the Gods and mortal men sprang from one source.

(ll. 109-120) First of all the deathless Gods who dwell on Olympus made a golden race of mortal men who lived in the time of Cronos when he was reigning in heaven. And they lived like Gods without sorrow of heart, remote and free from toil and grief: miserable age rested not on them; but with legs and arms never failing they made merry with feasting beyond the reach of all evils. When they died, it was as though they were overcome with sleep, and they had all good things; for the fruitful earth unforced bare them fruit abundantly and without stint. They dwelt in ease and peace upon their lands with many good things, rich in flocks and loved by the blessed Gods.

(ll. 121-139) But after earth had covered this generation -- they are called pure spirits dwelling on the earth, and are kindly, delivering from harm, and guardians of mortal men; for they roam everywhere over the earth, clothed in mist and keep watch on judgments and cruel deeds, givers of wealth; for this royal right also they received; -- then they who dwell on Olympus made a second generation which was of silver and less noble by far. It was like the golden race neither in body nor in spirit. A child was brought up at his good mother's side a hundred years, an utter simpleton, playing childishly in his own home. But when they were full grown and were come to the full measure of their prime, they lived only a little time in sorrow because of their foolishness, for they could not keep from sinning and from wronging one another, nor would they serve the immortals, nor sacrifice on the holy altars of the blessed ones as it is right for men to do wherever they dwell. Then Zeus the son of Cronos was angry and put them away, because they would not give honor to the blessed Gods who live on Olympus.

(ll. 140-155) But when earth had covered this generation also -- they are called blessed spirits of the underworld by men, and, though they are of second order, yet honor attends them also -- Zeus the Father made a third generation of mortal men, a brazen race, sprung from ash-trees (4); and it was in no way equal to the silver age, but was terrible and strong. They loved the lamentable works of Ares and deeds of violence; they ate no bread, but were hard of heart like adamant, fearful men. Great was their strength and unconquerable the arms which grew from their shoulders on their strong limbs. Their amour was of bronze, and their houses of bronze and of bronze were their implements: there was no black iron. These were destroyed by their own hands and passed to the dank house of chill Hades, and left no name: terrible though they were, Black Death seized them, and they left the bright light of the sun.

(ll. 156-169b) But when earth had covered this generation also, Zeus the son of Cronos made yet another, the fourth, upon the fruitful earth, which was nobler and more righteous, a God-like race of hero-men who are called demi-Gods, the race before our own, throughout the boundless earth. Grim war and dread battle destroyed a part of them, some in the land of Cadmus at seven- gated Thebe when they fought for the flocks of Oedipus, and some, when it had brought them in ships over the great sea gulf to Troy for rich-haired Helen's sake: there death's end enshrouded a part of them. But to the others father Zeus the son of Cronos gave a living and an abode apart from men, and made them dwell at the ends of earth. And they live untouched by sorrow in the islands of the blessed along the shore of deep swirling Ocean, happy heroes for whom the grain-giving earth bears honey-sweet fruit flourishing thrice a year, far from the deathless Gods, and Cronos rules over them (5); for the father of men and Gods released him from his bonds. And these last equally have honor and glory.

(ll. 169c-169d) And again far-seeing Zeus made yet another generation, the fifth, of men who are upon the bounteous earth.

(ll. 170-201) Thereafter, would that I was not among the men of the fifth generation, but either had died before or been born afterwards. For now truly is a race of iron, and men never rest from labor and sorrow by day, and from perishing by night; and the Gods shall lay sore trouble upon them. But, notwithstanding, even these shall have some good mingled with their evils. And Zeus will destroy this race of mortal men also when they come to have grey hair on the temples at their birth (6). The father will not agree with his children, nor the children with their father, nor guest with his host, nor comrade with comrade; nor will brother be dear to brother as aforetime. Men will dishonor their parents as they grow quickly old, and will carp at them, chiding them with bitter words, hard-hearted they, not knowing the fear of the Gods. They will not repay their aged parents the cost their nurture, for might shall be their right: and one man will sack another's city. There will be no favor for the man who keeps his oath or for the just or for the good; but rather men will praise the evil-doer and his violent dealing. Strength will be right and reverence will cease to be; and the wicked will hurt the worthy man, speaking false words against him, and will swear an oath upon them. Envy, foul-mouthed, delighting in evil, with scowling face, will go along with wretched men one and all. And then Aidos and Nemesis (7), with their sweet forms wrapped in white robes, will go from the wide-pathed earth and forsake mankind to join the company of the deathless Gods: and bitter sorrows will be left for mortal men, and there will be no help against evil.

(ll. 202-211) And now I will tell a fable for princes who themselves understand. Thus said the hawk to the nightingale with speckled neck, while he carried her high up among the clouds, gripped fast in his talons, and she, pierced by his crooked talons, cried pitifully. To her he spoke disdainfully: 'Miserable thing, why do you cry out? One far stronger than you now holds you fast and you must go wherever I take you, songstress as you are. And if I please I will make my meal of you, or let you go. He is a fool who tries to withstand the stronger, for he does not get the mastery and suffers pain besides his shame.' So said the swiftly flying hawk, the long- winged bird.

(ll. 212-224) But you, Perses, listen to right and do not foster violence; for violence is bad for a poor man. Even the prosperous cannot easily bear its burden, but is weighed down under it when he has fallen into delusion. The better path is to go by on the other side towards justice; for Justice beats Outrage when she comes at length to the end of the race. But only when he has suffered does the fool learn this. For Oath keeps pace with wrong judgments. There is a noise when Justice is being dragged in the way where those who devour bribes and give sentence with crooked judgments, take her. And she, wrapped in mist, follows to the city and haunts of the people, weeping, and bringing mischief to men, even to such as have driven her forth in that they did not deal straightly with her.

(ll. 225-237) But they who give straight judgments to strangers and to the men of the land, and go not aside from what is just, their city flourishes, and the people prosper in it: Peace, the nurse of children, is abroad in their land, and all-seeing Zeus never decrees cruel war against them. Neither famine nor disaster ever haunts men who do true justice; but light-heartedly they tend the fields which are all their care. The earth bears them victual in plenty, and on the mountains the oak bears acorns upon the top and bees in the midst. Their woolly sheep are laden with fleeces; their women bear children like their parents. They flourish continually with good things, and do not travel on ships, for the grain-giving earth bears them fruit.

(ll. 238-247) But for those who practice violence and cruel deeds far-seeing Zeus, the son of Cronos, ordains a punishment. Often even a whole city suffers for a bad man who sins and devises presumptuous deeds, and the son of Cronos lays great trouble upon the people, famine and plague together, so that the men perish away, and their women do not bear children, and their houses become few, through the contriving of Olympian Zeus. And again, at another time, the son of Cronos either destroys their wide army, or their walls, or else makes an end of their ships on the sea.

(ll. 248-264) You princes, mark well this punishment you also; for the deathless Gods are near among men and mark all those who oppress their fellows with crooked judgments, and reek not the anger of the Gods. For upon the bounteous earth Zeus has thrice ten thousand spirits, watchers of mortal men, and these keep watch on judgments and deeds of wrong as they roam, clothed in mist, all over the earth. And there is virgin Justice, the daughter of Zeus, who is honored and reverenced among the Gods who dwell on Olympus, and whenever anyone hurts her with lying slander, she sits beside her father, Zeus the son of Cronos, and tells him of men's wicked heart, until the people pay for the mad folly of their princes who, evilly minded, pervert judgment and give sentence crookedly. Keep watch against this, you princes, and make straight your judgments, you who devour bribes; put crooked judgments altogether from your thoughts.

(ll. 265-266) He does mischief to himself who does mischief to another, and evil planned harms the plotter most.

(ll. 267-273) The eye of Zeus, seeing all and understanding all, beholds these things too, if so he will, and fails not to mark what sort of justice is this that the city keeps within it. Now, therefore, may neither I myself be righteous among men, nor my son -- for then it is a bad thing to be righteous -- if indeed the unrighteous shall have the greater right. But I think that all-wise Zeus will not yet bring that to pass.

(ll. 274-285) But you, Perses, lay up these things within your heart and listen now to right, ceasing altogether to think of violence. For the son of Cronos has ordained this law for men, that fishes and beasts and winged fowls should devour one another, for right is not in them; but to mankind he gave right which proves far the best. For whoever knows the right and is ready to speak it, far-seeing Zeus gives him prosperity; but whoever deliberately lies in his witness and forswears himself, and so hurts Justice and sins beyond repair, that man's generation is left obscure thereafter. But the generation of the man who swears truly is better henceforward.

(ll. 286-292) To you, foolish Perses, I will speak good sense. Badness can be got easily and in shoals: the road to her is smooth, and she lives very near us. But between us and Goodness the Gods have placed the sweat of our brows: long and steep is the path that leads to her, and it is rough at the first; but when a man has reached the top, then is she easy to reach, though before that she was hard.

(ll. 293-319) That man is altogether best who considers all things himself and marks what will be better afterwards and at the end; and he, again, is good who listens to a good adviser; but whoever neither thinks for himself nor keeps in mind what another tells him, he is an unprofitable man. But do you at any rate, always remembering my charge, work; high-born Perses that Hunger may hate you, and venerable Demeter richly crowned may love you and fill your barn with food; for Hunger is altogether a meet comrade for the sluggard. Both Gods and men are angry with a man who lives idle, for in nature he is like the stingless drones that waste the labor of the bees, eating without working; but let it be your care to order your work properly, that in the right season your barns may be full of victual. Through work men grow rich in flocks and substance, and working they are much better loved by the immortals (8). Work is no disgrace: it is idleness which is a disgrace. But if you work, the idle will soon envy you as you grow rich, for fame and renown attend on wealth. And whatever be your lot, work is best for you, if you turn your misguided mind away from other men's property to your work and attend to your livelihood as I bid you. An evil shame is the needy man's companion, shame which both greatly harms and prospers men: shame is with poverty, but confidence with wealth.

(ll. 320-341) Wealth should not be seized: God-given wealth is much better; for it a man take great wealth violently and perforce, or if he steal it through his tongue, as often happens when gain deceives men's sense and dishonor tramples down honor, the Gods soon blot him out and make that man's house low, and wealth attends him only for a little time. Alike with him who does wrong to a suppliant or a guest, or who goes up to his brother's bed and commits unnatural sin in lying with his wife, or who infatuatedly offends against fatherless children, or who abuses his old father at the cheerless threshold of old age and attacks him with harsh words, truly Zeus himself is angry, and at the last lays on him a heavy requital for his evil doing. But do you turn your foolish heart altogether away from these things, and, as far as you are able, sacrifice to the deathless Gods purely and cleanly, and burn rich meats also, and at other times propitiate them with libations and incense, both when you go to bed and when the holy light has come back, that they may be gracious to you in heart and spirit, and so you may buy another's holding and not another yours.

(ll. 342-351) Call your friend to a feast; but leave your enemy alone; and especially call him who lives near you: for if any mischief happen in the place, neighbors come ungirt, but kinsmen stay to gird themselves (9). A bad neighbors as great a plague as a good one is a great blessing; he who enjoys a good neighbor has a precious possession. Not even an ox would die but for a bad neighbor. Take fair measure from your neighbor and pay him back fairly with the same measure, or better, if you can; so that if you are in need afterwards, you may find him sure.

(ll. 352-369) Do not get base gain: base gain is as bad as ruin. Be friends with the friendly, and visit him who visits you. Give to one who gives, but do not give to one who does not give. A man gives to the free-handed, but no one gives to the close- fisted. Give is a good girl, but Take is bad and she brings death. For the man who gives willingly, even though he gives a great thing, rejoices in his gift and is glad in heart; but whoever gives way to shamelessness and takes something himself, even though it be a small thing, it freezes his heart. He who adds to what he has will keep off bright-eyed hunger; for it you add only a little to a little and do this often, soon that little will become great. What a man has by him at home does not trouble him: it is better to have your stuff at home, for whatever is abroad may mean loss. It is a good thing to draw on what you have; but it grieves your heart to need something and not to have it, and I bid you mark this. Take your fill when the cask is first opened and when it is nearly spent, but midways be sparing: it is poor saving when you come to the lees.

(ll. 370-372) Let the wage promised to a friend be fixed; even with your brother smile -- and get a witness; for trust and mistrust, alike ruin men.

(ll. 373-375) Do not let a flaunting woman coax and cozen and deceive you: she is after your barn. The man who trusts womankind trust deceivers.

(ll. 376-380) There should be an only son, to feed his father's house, for so wealth will increase in the home; but if you leave a second son you should die old. Yet Zeus can easily give great wealth to a greater number. More hands mean more work and more increase.

(ll. 381-382) If your heart within you desires wealth, do these things and work with work upon work.

(ll. 383-404) When the Pleiades, daughters of Atlas, are rising (10), begin your harvest, and your plowing when they are going to set (11). Forty nights and days they are hidden and appear again as the year moves round, when first you sharpen your sickle. This is the law of the plains, and of those who live near the sea, and who inhabit rich country, the glens and dingles far from the tossing sea, -- strip to sow and strip to plough and strip to reap, if you wish to get in all Demeter's fruits in due season, and that each kind may grow in its season. Else, afterwards, you may chance to be in want, and go begging to other men's houses, but without avail; as you have already come to me. But I will give you no more nor give you further measure. Foolish Perses! Work the work which the Gods ordained for men, lest in bitter anguish of spirit you with your wife and children seek your livelihood amongst your neighbors, and they do not heed you. Two or three times, may be, you will succeed, but if you trouble them further, it will not avail you, and all your talk will be in vain, and your word-play unprofitable. Nay, I bid you find a way to pay your debts and avoid hunger.

(ll. 405-413) First of all, get a house, and a woman and an ox for the plow -- a slave woman and not a wife, to follow the oxen as well -- and make everything ready at home, so that you may not have to ask of another, and he refuses you, and so, because you are in lack, the season pass by and your work come to nothing. Do not put your work off till to-morrow and the day after; for a sluggish worker does not fill his barn, nor one who puts off his work: industry makes work go well, but a man who putts off work is always at hand-grips with ruin.

(ll. 414-447) When the piercing power and sultry heat of the sun abate, and almighty Zeus sends the autumn rains (12), and men's flesh comes to feel far easier, -- for then the star Sirius passes over the heads of men, who are born to misery, only a little while by day and takes greater share of night, -- then, when it showers its leaves to the ground and stops sprouting, the wood you cut with your axe is least liable to worm. Then remember to hew your timber: it is the season for that work. Cut a mortar (13) three feet wide and a pestle three cubits long, and an axle of seven feet, for it will do very well so; but if you make it eight feet long, you can cut a beetle (14) from it as well. Cut a felloe three spans across for a wagon of ten palms' width. Hew also many bent timbers, and bring home a plough-tree when you have found it, and look out on the mountain or in the field for one of holm-oak; for this is the strongest for oxen to plough with when one of Athena's handmen has fixed in the share-beam and fastened it to the pole with dowels. Get two ploughs ready work on them at home, one all of a piece, and the other jointed. It is far better to do this, for if you should break one of them, you can put the oxen to the other. Poles of laurel or elm are most free from worms, and a share-beam of oak and a plough-tree of holm-oak. Get two oxen, bulls of nine years; for their strength is unspent and they are in the prime of their age: they are best for work. They will not fight in the furrow and break the plough and then leave the work undone. Let a brisk fellow of forty years follow them, with a loaf of four quarters (15) and eight slices (16) for his dinner, one who will attend to his work and drive a straight furrow and is past the age for gaping after his fellows, but will keep his mind on his work. No younger man will be better than he at scattering the seed and avoiding double-sowing; for a man less staid gets disturbed, hankering after his fellows.

(ll. 448-457) Mark, when you hear the voice of the crane (17) who cries year by year from the clouds above, for she gives the signal for plowing and shows the season of rainy winter; but she vexes the heart of the man who has no oxen. Then is the time to feed up your horned oxen in the byre; for it is easy to say: 'Give me a yoke of oxen and a wagon,' and it is easy to refuse: 'I have work for my oxen.' The man who is rich in fancy thinks his wagon as good as built already -- the fool! He does not know that there are a hundred timbers to a wagon. Take care to lay these up beforehand at home.

(ll. 458-464) So soon as the time for plowing is proclaimed to men, then make haste, you and your slaves alike, in wet and in dry, to plow in the season for plowing, and bestir yourself early in the morning so that your fields may be full. Plow in the spring; but fallow broken up in the summer will not belie your hopes. Sow fallow land when the soil is still getting light: fallow land is a defender from harm and a soother of children.

(ll. 465-478) Pray to Zeus of the Earth and to pure Demeter to make Demeter's holy grain sound and heavy, when first you begin plowing, when you hold in your hand the end of the plow-tail and bring down your stick on the backs of the oxen as they draw on the pole-bar by the yoke-straps. Let a slave follow a little behind with a mattock and make trouble for the birds by hiding the seed; for good management is the best for mortal men as bad management is the worst. In this way your corn-ears will bow to the ground with fullness if the Olympian himself gives a good result at the last, and you will sweep the cobwebs from your bins and you will be glad, I wean, as you take of your garnered substance. And so you will have plenty till you come to grey (18) springtime, and will not look wistfully to others, but another shall be in need of your help.

(ll. 479-492) But if you plow the good ground at the solstice (19), you will reap sitting, grasping a thin crop in your hand, binding the sheaves awry, dust-covered, and not glad at all; so you will bring all home in a basket and not many will admire you. Yet the will of Zeus who holds the aegis is different at different times; and it is hard for mortal men to tell it; for if you should plow late, you may find this remedy -- when the cuckoo first calls (20) in the leaves of the oak and makes men glad all over the boundless earth, if Zeus should send rain on the third day and not cease until it rises neither above an ox's hoof nor falls short of it, then the late-plower will vie with the early. Keep all this well in mind, and fail not to mark grey spring as it comes and the season of rain.

(ll 493-501) Pass by the smithy and its crowded lounge in winter time when the cold keeps men from field work, -- for then an industrious man can greatly prosper his house -- lest bitter winter catch you helpless and poor and you chafe a swollen foot with a shrunk hand. The idle man who waits on empty hope, lacking a livelihood, lays to heart mischief-making; it is not an wholesome hope that accompanies a need man who lolls at ease while he has no sure livelihood.

(ll. 502-503) While it is yet midsummer command your slaves: 'It will not always be summer, build barns.'

(ll. 504-535) Avoid the month Lenaeon (21), wretched days, all of them fit to skin an ox, and the frosts which are cruel when Boreas blows over the earth. He blows across horse-breeding Thrace upon the wide sea and stirs it up, while earth and the forest howl. On many a high-leafed oak and thick pine he falls and brings them to the bounteous earth in mountain glens: then all the immense wood roars and the beasts shudder and put their tails between their legs, even those whose hide is covered with fur; for with his bitter blast he blows even through them although they are shaggy-breasted. He goes even through an ox's hide; it does not stop him. Also he blows through the goat's fine hair. But through the fleeces of sheep, because their wool is abundant, the keen wind Boreas pierces not at all; but it makes the old man curved as a wheel. And it does not blow through the tender maiden who stays indoors with her dear mother, unlearned as yet in the works of golden Aphrodite, and who washes her soft body and anoints herself with oil and lies down in an inner room within the house, on a winter's day when the Boneless One (22) gnaws his foot in his fireless house and wretched home; for the sun shows him no pastures to make for, but goes to and fro over the land and city of dusky men (23), and shines more sluggishly upon the whole race of the Hellenes. Then the horned and unhorned denizens of the wood, with teeth chattering pitifully, flee through the copses and glades, and all, as they seek shelter, have this one care, to gain thick coverts or some hollow rock. Then, like the Three-legged One (24) whose back is broken and whose head looks down upon the ground, like him, I say, they wander to escape the white snow.

(ll. 536-563) Then put on, as I bid you, a soft coat and a tunic to the feet to shield your body, -- and you should weave thick woof on thin warp. In this clothe yourself so that your hair may keep still and not bristle and stand upon end all over your body.

Lace on your feet close-fitting boots of the hide of a slaughtered ox, thickly lined with felt inside. And when the season of frost comes on, stitch together skins of firstling kids with ox-sinew, to put over your back and to keep off the rain. On your head above wear a shaped cap of felt to keep your ears from getting wet, for the dawn is chill when Boreas has once made his onslaught, and at dawn a fruitful mist is spread over the earth from starry heaven upon the fields of blessed men: it is drawn from the ever flowing rivers and is raised high above the earth by windstorm, and sometimes it turns to rain towards evening, and sometimes to wind when Thracian Boreas huddles the thick clouds. Finish your work and return home ahead of him, and do not let the dark cloud from heaven wrap round you and make your body clammy and soak your clothes. Avoid it; for this is the hardest month, wintry, hard for sheep and hard for men. In this season let your oxen have half their usual food, but let your man have more; for the helpful nights are long. Observe all this until the year is ended and you have nights and days of equal length, and Earth, the mother of all, bears again her various fruit.

(ll. 564-570) When Zeus has finished sixty wintry days after the solstice, then the star Arcturus (25) leaves the holy stream of Ocean and first rises brilliant at dusk. After him the shrilly wailing daughter of Pandion, the swallow, appears to men when spring is just beginning. Before she comes, prune the vines, for it is best so.

(ll. 571-581) But when the House-carrier (26) climbs up the plants from the earth to escape the Pleiades, then it is no longer the season for digging vineyards, but to whet your sickles and rouse up your slaves. Avoid shady seats and sleeping until dawn in the harvest season, when the sun scorches the body. Then be busy, and bring home your fruits, getting up early to make your livelihood sure. For dawn takes away a third part of your work, dawn advances a man on his journey and advances him in his work, -- dawn which appears and sets many men on their road, and puts yokes on many oxen.

(ll. 582-596) But when the artichoke flowers (27), and the chirping grass-hopper sits in a tree and pours down his shrill song continually from under his wings in the season of wearisome heat, then goats are plumpest and wine sweetest; women are most wanton, but men are feeblest, because Sirius parches head and knees and the skin is dry through heat. But at that time let me have a shady rock and wine of Biblis, a clot of curds and milk of drained goats with the flesh of an heifer fed in the woods, that has never calved, and of firstling kids; then also let me drink bright wine, sitting in the shade, when my heart is satisfied with food, and so, turning my head to face the fresh Zephyr, from the ever flowing spring which pours down unfouled thrice pour an offering of water, but make a fourth libation of wine.

(ll. 597-608) Set your slaves to winnow Demeter's holy grain, when strong Orion (28) first appears, on a smooth threshing-floor in an airy place. Then measure it and store it in jars. And as soon as you have safely stored all your stuff indoors, I bid you put your bondman out of doors and look out for a servant-girl with no children; -- for a servant with a child to nurse is troublesome. And look after the dog with jagged teeth; do not grudge him his food, or some time the Day-sleeper (29) may take your stuff. Bring in fodder and litter so as to have enough for your oxen and mules. After that, let your men rest their poor knees and unyoke your pair of oxen.

(ll. 609-617) But when Orion and Sirius are come into mid-heaven, and rosy-fingered Dawn sees Arcturus (30), then cut off all the grape-clusters, Perses, and bring them home. Show them to the sun ten days and ten nights: then cover them over for five, and on the sixth day draw off into vessels the gifts of joyful Dionysus. But when the Pleiades and Hades and strong Orion begin to set (31), then remember to plow in season: and so the completed year (32) will fitly pass beneath the earth.

(ll. 618-640) But if desire for uncomfortable sea-faring seize you; when the Pleiades plunge into the misty sea (33) to escape Orion's rude strength, then truly gales of all kinds rage. Then keep ships no longer on the sparkling sea, but bethink you to till the land as I bid you. Haul up your ship upon the land and pack it closely with stones all around to keep off the power of the winds which blow damply, and draw out the bilge-plug so that the rain of heaven may not rot it. Put away all the tackle and fittings in your house, and stow the wings of the sea-going ship neatly, and hang up the well-shaped rudder over the smoke. You yourself wait until the season for sailing is come, and then haul your swift ship down to the sea and stow a convenient cargo in it, so that you may bring home profit, even as your father and mine, foolish Perses, used to sail on shipboard because he lacked sufficient livelihood. And one day he came to this very place crossing over a great stretch of sea; he left Aeolian Cyme and fled, not from riches and substance, but from wretched poverty which Zeus lays upon men, and he settled near Helicon in a miserable hamlet, Ascra, which is bad in winter, sultry in summer, and good at no time.

(ll. 641-645) But you, Perses, remember all works in their season but sailing especially. Admire a small ship, but put your freight in a large one; for the greater the lading, the greater will be your piled gain, if only the winds will keep back their harmful gales.

(ll. 646-662) If ever you turn your misguided heart to trading and with to escape from debt and joyless hunger, I will show you the measures of the loud-roaring sea, though I have no skill in sea-faring nor in ships; for never yet have I sailed by ship over the wide sea, but only to Euboea from Aulis where the Achaeans once stayed through much storm when they had gathered a great host from divine Hellas for Troy, the land of fair women. Then I crossed over to Chalcis, to the games of wise Amphidamas where the sons of the great-hearted Hero proclaimed and appointed prizes. And there I boast that I gained the victory with a song and carried off a handled tripod which I dedicated to the Muses of Helicon, in the place where they first set me in the way of clear song. Such is all my experience of many-pegged ships; nevertheless I will tell you the will of Zeus who holds the aegis; for the Muses have taught me to sing in marvelous song.

(ll. 663-677) Fifty days after the solstice (34), when the season of wearisome heat is come to an end, is the right time for me to go sailing. Then you will not wreck your ship, nor will the sea destroy the sailors, unless Poseidon the Earth-Shaker be set upon it, or Zeus, the king of the deathless Gods, wish to slay them; for the issues of good and evil alike are with them. At that time the winds are steady, and the sea is harmless. Then trust in the winds without care, and haul your swift ship down to the sea and put all the freight no board; but make all haste you can to return home again and do not wait till the time of the new wine and autumn rain and oncoming storms with the fierce gales of Notus who accompanies the heavy autumn rain of Zeus and stirs up the sea and makes the deep dangerous.

(ll. 678-694) Another time for men to go sailing is in spring when a man first sees leaves on the topmost shoot of a fig-tree as large as the foot-print that a cow makes; then the sea is passable, and this is the spring sailing time. For my part I do not praise it, for my heart does not like it. Such a sailing is snatched, and you will hardly avoid mischief. Yet in their ignorance men do even this, for wealth means life to poor mortals; but it is fearful to die among the waves. But I bid you consider all these things in your heart as I say. Do not put all your goods in hallow ships; leave the greater part behind, and put the lesser part on board; for it is a bad business to meet with disaster among the waves of the sea, as it is bad if you put too great a load on your wagon and break the axle, and your goods are spoiled. Observe due measure: and proportion is best in all things.

(ll. 695-705) Bring home a wife to your house when you are of the right age, while you are not far short of thirty years nor much above; this is the right age for marriage. Let your wife have been grown up four years, and marry her in the fifth. Marry a maiden, so that you can teach her careful ways, and especially marry one who lives near you, but look well about you and see that your marriage will not be a joke to your neighbors. For a man wins nothing better than a good wife, and, again, nothing worse than a bad one, a greedy soul who roasts her man without fire, strong though he may be, and brings him to a raw (35) old age.

(ll. 706-714) Be careful to avoid the anger of the deathless Gods. Do not make a friend equal to a brother; but if you do, do not wrong him first, and do not lie to please the tongue. But if he wrongs you first, offending either in word or in deed, remember to repay him double; but if he ask you to be his friend again and be ready to give you satisfaction, welcome him. He is a worthless man who makes now one and now another his friend; but as for you, do not let your face put your heart to shame (36).

(ll. 715-716) Do not get a name either as lavish or as churlish; as a friend of rogues or as a slanderer of good men.

(ll. 717-721) Never dare to taunt a man with deadly poverty which eats out the heart; it is sent by the deathless Gods. The best treasure a man can have is a sparing tongue, and the greatest pleasure, one that moves orderly; for if you speak evil, you yourself will soon be worse spoken of.

(ll. 722-723) Do not be boorish at a common feast where there are many guests; the pleasure is greatest and the expense is least (37).

(ll. 724-726) Never pour a libation of sparkling wine to Zeus after dawn with unwashed hands, nor to others of the deathless Gods; else do they not hear your prayers but spit them back.

(ll. 727-732) Do not stand upright facing the sun when you make water, but remember to do this when he has set towards his rising. And do not make water as you go, whether on the road or off the road, and do not uncover yourself: the nights belong to the blessed Gods. A scrupulous man who has a wise heart sits down or goes to the wall of an enclosed court.

(ll. 733-736) Do not expose yourself befouled by the fireside in your house, but avoid this. Do not beget children when you are come back from ill-omened burial, but after a festival of the Gods.

(ll. 737-741) Never cross the sweet-flowing water of ever-rolling rivers afoot until you have prayed, gazing into the soft flood, and washed your hands in the clear, lovely water. Whoever crosses a river with hands unwashed of wickedness; the Gods are angry with him and bring trouble upon him afterwards.

(ll. 742-743) At a cheerful festival of the Gods do not cut the withered from the quick upon that which has five branches (38) with bright steel.

(ll. 744-745) Never put the ladle upon the mixing-bowl at a wine party, for malignant ill-luck is attached to that.

(ll. 746-747) When you are building a house, do not leave it rough-hewn, or a cawing crow may settle on it and croak.

(ll. 748-749) Take nothing to eat or to wash with from uncharmed pots, for in them there is mischief.

(ll. 750-759) Do not let a boy of twelve years sit on things which may not be moved (39), for that is bad, and makes a man unmanly; nor yet a child of twelve months, for that has the same effect. A man should not clean his body with water in which a woman has washed, for there is bitter mischief in that also for a time. When you come upon a burning sacrifice, do not make a mock of mysteries, for Heaven is angry at this also. Never make water in the mouths of rivers which flow to the sea, nor yet in springs; but be careful to avoid this. And do not ease yourself in them: it is not well to do this.

(ll. 760-763) So do: and avoid the talk of men. For talk is mischievous, light, and easily raised, but hard to bear and difficult to be rid of. Talk never wholly dies away when many people voice her: even Talk is in some ways divine.

(ll. 765-767) Mark the days which come from Zeus, duly telling your slaves of them, and that the thirtieth day of the month is best for one to look over the work and to deal out supplies.

(ll. 769-768) (40) For these are days which come from Zeus the all-wise, when men discern aright.

(ll. 770-779) To begin with, the first, the fourth, and the seventh -- on which Leto bare Apollo with the blade of gold -- each is a holy day. The eighth and the ninth, two days at least of the waxing month (41), are especially good for the works of man. Also the eleventh and twelfth are both excellent, alike for shearing sheep and for reaping the kindly fruits; but the twelfth is much better than the eleventh, for on it the airy-swinging spider spins its web in full day, and then the Wise One (42), gathers her pile. On that day woman should set up her loom and get forward with her work.

(ll. 780-781) Avoid the thirteenth of the waxing month for beginning to sow: yet it is the best day for setting plants.

(ll. 782-789) The sixth of the mid-month is very unfavorable for plants, but is good for the birth of males, though unfavorable for a girl either to be born at all or to be married. Nor is the first sixth a fit day for a girl to be born, but a kindly for gelding kids and sheep and for fencing in a sheep-cote. It is favorable for the birth of a boy, but such will be fond of sharp speech, lies, and cunning words, and stealthy converse.

(ll. 790-791) On the eighth of the month geld the boar and loud-bellowing bull, but hard-working mules on the twelfth.

(ll. 792-799) On the great twentieth, in full day, a wise man should be born. Such a one is very sound-witted. The tenth is favorable for a male to be born; but, for a girl, the fourth day of the mid-month. On that day tame sheep and shambling, horned oxen, and the sharp-fanged dog and hardy mules to the touch of the hand. But take care to avoid troubles which eat out the heart on the fourth of the beginning and ending of the month; it is a day very fraught with fate.

(ll. 800-801) On the fourth of the month bring home your bride, but choose the omens which are best for this business.

(ll. 802-804) Avoid fifth days: they are unkindly and terrible. On a fifth day, they say, the Erinyes assisted at the birth of Horcus (Oath) whom Eris (Strife) bare to trouble the forsworn.

(ll. 805-809) Look about you very carefully and throw out Demeter's holy grain upon the well-rolled (43) threshing floor on the seventh of the mid-month. Let the woodman cut beams for house building and plenty of ships' timbers, such as are suitable for ships. On the fourth day begin to build narrow ships.

(ll. 810-813) The ninth of the mid-month improves towards evening; but the first ninth of all is quite harmless for men. It is a good day on which to beget or to be born both for a male and a female: it is never a wholly evil day.

(ll. 814-818) Again, few know that the twenty-seventh of the month is best for opening a wine-jar, and putting yokes on the necks of oxen and mules and swift-footed horses, and for hauling a swift ship of many thwarts down to the sparkling sea; few call it by its right name.

(ll. 819-821) On the fourth day open a jar. The fourth of the mid-month is a day holy above all. And again, few men know that the fourth day after the twentieth is best while it is morning: towards evening it is less good.

(ll. 822-828) These days are a great blessing to men on earth; but the rest are changeable, luckless, and bring nothing. Everyone praises a different day but few know their nature. Sometimes a day is a stepmother, sometimes a mother. That man is happy and lucky in them who knows all these things and does his work without offending the deathless Gods, who discerns the omens of birds and avoids transgressions.

ENDNOTES:

(1) That is, the poor man's fare, like 'bread and cheese'.

(2) The All-endowed.

(3) The jar or casket contained the gifts of the Gods mentioned in l.82.

(4) Eustathius refers to Hesiod as stating that men sprung 'from oaks and stones and ashtrees'. Proclus believed that the Nymphs called Meliae ("Theogony", 187) are intended. Goettling would render: 'A race terrible because of their (ashen) spears.'

(5) Preserved only by Proclus, from whom some inferior MSS. Have copied the verse. The four following lines occur only in Geneva Papyri No. 94. For the restoration of ll. 169b-c see "Class. Quart." vii. 219-220. (NOTE: Mr. Evelyn-White means that the version quoted by Proclus stops at this point, then picks up at l. 170. -- DBK).

(6) i.e. the race will so degenerate that at the last even a new-born child will show the marks of old age.

(7) Aidos, as a quality, is that feeling of reverence or shame which restrains men from wrong: Nemesis is the feeling of righteous indignation aroused especially by the sight of the wicked in undeserved prosperity (cf. "Psalms", lxxii. 1-19).

(8) The alternative version is: 'and, working, you will be much better loved both by Gods and men; for they greatly dislike the idle.'

(9) i.e. neighbors come at once and without making preparations, but kinsmen by marriage (who live at a distance) have to prepare, and so are long in coming.

(10) Early in May.

(11) In November.

(12) In October.

(13) For pounding corn.

(14) A mallet for breaking clods after plowing.

(15) The loaf is a flattish cake with two intersecting lines scored on its upper surface which divide it into four equal parts.

(16) The meaning is obscure. A scholiast renders 'giving eight mouthfuls'; but the elder Philostratus uses the word in contrast to 'leavened'.

(17) About the middle of November.

(18) Spring is so described because the buds have not yet cast their iron-grey husks.

(19) In December.

(20) In March.

(21) The latter part of January and earlier part of February.

(22) i.e. the octopus or cuttle.

(23) i.e. the darker-skinned people of Africa, the Egyptians or Aethiopians.

(24) i.e. an old man walking with a staff (the 'third leg' – as in the riddle of the Sphinx).

(25) February to March.

(26) i.e. the snail. The season is the middle of May.

(27) In June.

(28) July.

(29) i.e. a robber.

(30) September.

(31) The end of October.

(32) That is, the succession of stars which make up the full year.

(33) The end of October or beginning of November.

(34) July-August.

(35) i.e. untimely, premature. Juvenal similarly speaks of 'cruda senectus' (caused by gluttony).

(36) The thought is parallel to that of 'O, what a goodly outside falsehood hath.'

(37) The 'common feast' is one to which all present subscribe. Theognis (line 495) says that one of the chief pleasures of a banquet is the general conversation. Hence the present passage means that such a feast naturally costs little, while the many present will make pleasurable conversation.

(38) i.e. 'do not cut your finger-nails'.

(39) i.e. things which it would be sacrilege to disturb, such as tombs.

(40) H.G. Evelyn-White prefers to switch ll. 768 and 769, reading l. 769 first then l. 768. -- DBK

(41) The month is divided into three periods, the waxing, the mid-month, and the waning, which answer to the phases of the moon.

(42) i.e. the ant.

(43) Such seems to be the meaning here, though the epithet is otherwise rendered 'well-rounded'. Corn was threshed by means of a sleigh with two runners having three or four rollers between them like the modern Egyptian "nurag."

Appendix II:
The Theogony of Hesiod
translated by Hugh G. Evelyn-White (1914)
edited by Timothy Jay Alexander

(ll. 1-25) From the Heliconian Muses let us begin to sing, who hold the great and holy mount of Helicon, and dance on soft feet about the deep-blue spring and the altar of the almighty son of Cronos, and, when they have washed their tender bodies in Permessus or in the Horse's Spring or Olmeius, make their fair, lovely dances upon highest Helicon and move with vigorous feet. Thence they arise and go abroad by night, veiled in thick mist, and utter their song with lovely voice, praising Zeus the aegis-holder and queenly Hera of Argos who walks on golden sandals and the daughter of Zeus the aegis-holder bright-eyed Athena, and Phoebus Apollo, and Artemis who delights in arrows, and Poseidon the earth-holder who shakes the earth, and reverend Themis and quick-glancing (1) Aphrodite, and Hebe with the crown of gold, and fair Dione, Leto, Iapetus, and Cronos the crafty counselor, Eos and great Helios and bright Selene, Earth too, and great Oceanus, and dark Night, and the holy race of all the other deathless ones that are for ever. And one day they taught Hesiod glorious song while he was shepherding his lambs under holy Helicon, and this word first the Goddesses said to me -- the Muses of Olympus, daughters of Zeus who holds the aegis:

(ll. 26-28) 'Shepherds of the wilderness, wretched things of shame, mere bellies, we know how to speak many false things as though they were true; but we know, when we will, to utter true things."

(ll. 29-35) So said the ready-voiced daughters of great Zeus, and they plucked and gave me a rod, a shoot of sturdy laurel, a marvelous thing, and breathed into me a divine voice to celebrate things that shall be and things there were aforetime; and they bade me sing of the race of the blessed Gods that are eternally, but ever to sing of themselves both first and last. But why all this about oak or stone? (2)

(ll. 36-52) Come thou, let us begin with the Muses who gladden the great spirit of their father Zeus in Olympus with their songs, telling of things that are and that shall be and that were aforetime with consenting voice. Unwearyingly flows the sweet sound from their lips, and the house of their father Zeus the loud-thunderer is glad at the lily-like voice of the Goddesses as it spread abroad, and the peaks of snowy Olympus resound, and the homes of the immortals. And they uttering their immortal voice, celebrate in song first of all the reverend race of the Gods from the beginning, those whom Earth and wide Heaven begot, and the Gods sprung of these, givers of good things. Then, next, the Goddesses sing of Zeus, the father of Gods and men, as they begin and end their strain, how much he is the most excellent among the Gods and supreme in power. And again, they chant the race of men and strong giants, and gladden the heart of Zeus within Olympus, -- the Olympian Muses, daughters of Zeus the aegis-holder.

(ll. 53-74) Those in Pieria did Mnemosyne (Memory), who reigns over the hills of Eleuther, bear of union with the father, the son of Cronos, a forgetting of ills and a rest from sorrow. For nine nights did wise Zeus lie with her, entering her holy bed remote from the immortals. And when a year was passed and the seasons came round as the months waned, and many days were accomplished, she bears nine daughters, all of one mind, whose hearts are set upon song and their spirit free from care, a little way from the topmost peak of snowy Olympus. There are their bright dancing-places and beautiful homes, and beside them the Graces and Himerus (Desire) live in delight. And they, uttering through their lips a lovely voice, sing the laws of all and the goodly ways of the immortals, uttering their lovely voice. Then went they to Olympus, delighting in their sweet voice, with heavenly song, and the dark earth resounded about them as they chanted, and a lovely sound rose up beneath their feet as they went to their father. And he was reigning in heaven, himself holding the lightning and glowing thunderbolt, when he had overcome by might his father Cronos; and he distributed fairly to the immortals their portions and declared their privileges.

(ll. 75-103) These things, then, the Muses sang who dwell on Olympus, nine daughters begotten by great Zeus, Cleio and Euterpe, Thaleia,

Melpomene and Terpsichore, and Erato and Polyhymnia and Urania and Calliope (3), who is the chiefest of them all, for she attends on worshipful princes: whomsoever of heaven-nourished princes the daughters of great Zeus honor, and behold him at his birth, they pour sweet dew upon his tongue, and from his lips flow gracious words. All the people look towards him while he settles causes with true judgments: and he, speaking surely, would soon make wise end even of a great quarrel; for therefore are there princes wise in heart, because when the people are being misguided in their assembly, they set right the matter again with ease, persuading them with gentle words. And when he passes through a gathering, they greet him as a God with gentle reverence, and he is conspicuous amongst the assembled: such is the holy gift of the Muses to men. For it is through the Muses and far-shooting Apollo that there are singers and harpers upon the earth; but princes are of Zeus, and happy is he whom the Muses love: sweet flows speech from his mouth. For though a man have sorrow and grief in his newly-troubled soul and live in dread because his heart is distressed, yet, when a singer, the servant of the Muses, chants the glorious deeds of men of old and the blessed Gods who inhabit Olympus, at once he forgets his heaviness and remembers not his sorrows at all; but the gifts of the Goddesses soon turn him away from these.

(ll. 104-115) Hail, children of Zeus! Grant lovely song and celebrate the holy race of the deathless Gods who are for ever, those that were born of Earth and starry Heaven and gloomy Night and them that briny Sea did rear. Tell how at the first Gods and earth came to be, and rivers, and the boundless sea with its raging swell, and the gleaming stars, and the wide heaven above, and the Gods who were born of them, givers of good things, and how they divided their wealth, and how they shared their honors amongst them, and also how at the first they took many-folded Olympus. These things declare to me from the beginning, ye Muses who dwell in the house of Olympus, and tell me which of them first came to be.

(ll. 116-138) Verily at the first Chaos came to be, but next wide-bosomed Earth, the ever-sure foundations of all (4) the deathless ones who hold the peaks of snowy Olympus, and dim Tartarus in the depth of the wide-pathed Earth, and Eros (Love), fairest among the deathless Gods, who unnerves the limbs and overcomes the mind and wise counsels of all Gods and all men within them. From Chaos came forth Erebus and black Night; but of Night were born Ether (5) and Day, whom she conceived and bear from union in love with Erebus. And Earth first bear starry Heaven, equal to herself, to cover her on every side, and to be an ever-sure abiding-place for the blessed Gods. And she brought forth long Hills, graceful haunts of the Goddess-Nymphs who dwell amongst the glens of the hills. She bears also the fruitless deep with his raging swell, Pontus, without sweet union of love. But afterwards she lay with Heaven and bear deep-swirling Oceanus, Coeus and Crius and Hyperion and Iapetus, Theia and Rhea, Themis and Mnemosyne and gold-crowned Phoebe and lovely Tethys. After them was born Cronos the wily, youngest and most terrible of her children, and he hated his lusty sire.

(ll. 139-146) And again, she bear the Cyclopes, overbearing in spirit, Brontes, and Steropes and stubborn-hearted Arges (6), who gave Zeus the thunder and made the thunderbolt: in all else they were like the Gods, but one eye only was set in the midst of their fore-heads. And they were surnamed Cyclopes (Orb-eyed) because one orbed eye was set in their foreheads. Strength and might and craft were in their works.

(ll. 147-163) And again, three other sons were born of Earth and Heaven, great and doughty beyond telling, Cottus and Briareos and Gyes, presumptuous children. From their shoulders sprang an hundred arms, not to be approached, and each had fifty heads upon his shoulders on their strong limbs, and irresistible was the stubborn strength that was in their great forms. For of all the children that were born of Earth and Heaven, these were the most terrible, and they were hated by their own father from the first.
And he used to hide them all away in a secret place of Earth so soon as each was born, and would not suffer them to come up into the light: and Heaven rejoiced in his evil doing. But vast Earth groaned within, being straitened, and she made the element of grey flint and shaped a great sickle, and told her plan to her dear sons. And she spoke, cheering them, while she was vexed in her dear heart:

(ll. 164-166) 'My children, gotten of a sinful father, if you will obey me, we should punish the vile outrage of your father; for he first thought of doing shameful things.'

(ll. 167-169) So she said; but fear seized them all, and none of them uttered a word. But great Cronos the wily took courage and answered his dear mother:

(ll. 170-172) 'Mother, I will undertake to do this deed, for I reverence not our father of evil name, for he first thought of doing shameful things.'

(ll. 173-175) So he said: and vast Earth rejoiced greatly in spirit, and set and hid him in an ambush, and put in his hands a jagged sickle, and revealed to him the whole plot.

(ll. 176-206) And Heaven came, bringing on night and longing for love, and he lay about Earth spreading himself full upon her (7).

Then the son from his ambush stretched forth his left hand and in his right took the great long sickle with jagged teeth, and swiftly lopped off his own father's members and cast them away to fall behind him. And not vainly did they fall from his hand; for all the bloody drops that gushed forth Earth received, and as the seasons moved round she bear the strong Erinyes and the great Giants with gleaming armor, holding long spears in their hands and the Nymphs whom they call Meliae (8) all over the boundless earth. And so soon as he had cut off the members with flint and cast them from the land into the surging sea, they were swept away over the main a long time: and a white foam spread around them from the immortal flesh, and in it there grew a maiden. First she drew near holy Cythera, and from there, afterwards, she came to sea-girt Cyprus, and came forth an awful and lovely Goddess, and grass grew up about her beneath her shapely feet. Her Gods and men call Aphrodite, and the foam-born Goddess and rich-crowned Cytherea, because she grew amid the foam, and Cytherea because she reached Cythera, and Cyprogenes because she was born in billowy Cyprus, and Philommedes (9) because sprang from the members. And with her went Eros, and comely Desire followed her at her birth at the first and as she went into the assembly of the Gods. This honor she has from the beginning, and this is the portion allotted to her amongst men and undying Gods, -- the whisperings of maidens and smiles and deceits with sweet delight and love and graciousness.

(ll. 207-210) But these sons whom be begot himself great Heaven used to call Titans (Strainers) in reproach, for he said that they strained and did presumptuously a fearful deed, and that vengeance for it would come afterwards.

(ll. 211-225) And Night bear hateful Doom and black Fate and Death, and she bear Sleep and the tribe of Dreams. And again the Goddess murky Night, though she lay with none, bear Blame and painful Woe, and the Hesperides who guard the rich, golden apples and the trees bearing fruit beyond glorious Ocean. Also she bear the Destinies and ruthless avenging Fates, Clotho and Lachesis and Atropos (10), who gives men at their birth both evil and good to have, and they pursue the transgressions of men and of Gods: and these Goddesses never cease from their dread anger until they punish the sinner with a sore penalty. Also deadly Night bear Nemesis (Indignation) to afflict mortal men, and after her, Deceit and Friendship and hateful Age and hard-hearted Strife.

(ll. 226-232) But abhorred Strife bear painful Toil and Forgetfulness and Famine and tearful Sorrows, Fightings also, Battles, Murders, Manslaughters, Quarrels, Lying Words, Disputes, Lawlessness and Ruin, all of one nature, and Oath who most troubles men upon earth when anyone willfully swears a false oath.

(ll. 233-239) And Sea begat Nereus, the eldest of his children, who is true and lies not: and men call him the Old Man because he is trusty and gentle and does not forget the laws of righteousness, but thinks just and kindly thoughts. And yet again he got great Thaumas and proud Phoreys, being mated with Earth, and fair-cheeked Ceto and Eurybia who has a heart of flint within her.

(ll. 240-264) And of Nereus and rich-haired Doris, daughter of Ocean the perfect river, were born children (11), passing lovely amongst Goddesses, Ploto, Eucrante, Sao, and Amphitrite, and Eudora, and Thetis, Galene and Glauce, Cymothoe, Speo, Thoe and lovely Halie, and Pasithea, and Erato, and rosy-armed Eunice, and gracious Melite, and Eulimene, and Agaue, Doto, Proto, Pherusa, and Dynamene, and Nisaea, and Actaea, and Protomedea, Doris, Panopea, and comely Galatea, and lovely Hippothoe, and rosy-armed Hipponoe, and Cymodoce who with Cymatolege (12) and Amphitrite easily calms the waves upon the misty sea and the blasts of raging winds, and Cymo, and Eione, and rich-crowned Alimede, and Glauconome, fond of laughter, and Pontoporea, Leagore, Euagore, and Laomedea, and Polynoe, and Autonoe, and Lysianassa, and Euarne, lovely of shape and without blemish of form, and Psamathe of charming figure and divine Menippe, Neso, Eupompe, Themisto, Pronoe, and Nemertes (13) who has the nature of her deathless father. These fifty daughters sprang from blameless Nereus, skilled in excellent crafts.

(ll. 265-269) And Thaumas wedded Electra the daughter of deep- flowing Ocean, and she bear him swift Iris and the long-haired Harpies, Aello (Storm-swift) and Ocypetes (Swift-flier) who on their swift wings keep pace with the blasts of the winds and the birds; for quick as time they dart along.

(ll 270-294) And again, Ceto bear to Phoreys the fair-cheeked Graiae, sisters grey from their birth: and both deathless Gods and men who walk on earth call them Graiae, Pemphredo well-clad, and saffron-robed Enyo, and the Gorgons who dwell beyond glorious Ocean in the frontier land towards Night where are the clear- voiced Hesperides, Sthenno, and Euryale, and Medusa who suffered a woeful fate: she was mortal, but the two were undying and grew not old. With her lay the Dark-haired One (14) in a soft meadow amid spring flowers. And when Perseus cut off her head, there sprang forth great Chrysaor and the horse Pegasus who is so called because he was born near the springs (pegae) of Ocean; and that other, because he held a golden blade (aor) in his hands. Now Pegasus flew away and left the earth, the mother of flocks, and came to the deathless Gods: and he dwells in the house of Zeus and brings to wise Zeus the thunder and lightning. But Chrysaor was joined in love to Callirrhoe, the daughter of glorious Ocean, and begot three-headed Geryones. Him mighty Heracles slew in sea-girt Erythea by his shambling oxen on that day when he drove the wide-browed oxen to holy Tiryns, and had crossed the ford of Ocean and killed Orthus and Eurytion the herdsman in the dim stead out beyond glorious Ocean.

(ll. 295-305) And in a hollow cave she bear another monster, irresistible, in no wise like either to mortal men or to the undying Gods, even the Goddess fierce Echidna who is half a nymph with glancing eyes and fair cheeks, and half again a huge snake, great and awful, with speckled skin, eating raw flesh beneath the secret parts of the holy earth. And there she has a cave deep down under a hollow rock far from the deathless Gods and mortal man. There, then, did the Gods appoint her a glorious house to dwell in: and she keeps guard in Arima beneath the earth, grim Echidna, a nymph who dies not nor grows old all her days.

(ll. 306-332) Men say that Typhaon the terrible, outrageous and lawless, was joined in love to her, the maid with glancing eyes. So she conceived and brought forth fierce offspring; first she bear Orthus the hound of Geryones, and then again she bear a second, a monster not to be overcome and that may not be described, Cerberus who eats raw flesh, the brazen-voiced hound of Hades, fifty-headed, relentless and strong. And again she bore a third, the evil-minded Hydra of Lerna, whom the Goddess, white-armed Hera nourished, being angry beyond measure with the mighty Heracles. And her Heracles, the son of Zeus, of the house of Amphitryon, together with warlike Iolaus, destroyed with the unpitying sword through the plans of Athena the spoil-driver. She was the mother of Chimaera who breathed raging fire, a creature fearful, great, swift-footed and strong, who had three heads, one of a grim-eyed lion; in her hinder-part, a dragon; and in her middle, a goat, breathing forth a fearful blast of blazing fire. Her did Pegasus and noble Bellerophon slay; but Echidna was subject in love to Orthus and brought forth the deadly Sphinx which destroyed the Cadmeans, and the Nemean lion, which Hera, the good wife of Zeus, brought up and made to haunt the hills of Nemea, a plague to men. There he preyed upon the tribes of her own people and had power over Tretus of Nemea and Apesas: yet the strength of stout Heracles overcame him.

(ll. 333-336) And Ceto was joined in love to Phorcys and bear her youngest, the awful snake who guards the apples all of gold in the secret places of the dark earth at its great bounds. This is the offspring of Ceto and Phoreys.

(ll. 334-345) And Tethys bear to Ocean eddying rivers, Nilus, and Alpheus, and deep-swirling Eridanus, Strymon, and Meander, and the fair stream of Ister, and Phasis, and Rhesus, and the silver eddies of Achelous, Nessus, and Rhodius, Haliacmon, and Heptaporus, Granicus, and Aesepus, and holy Simois, and Peneus, and Hermus, and Caicus fair stream, and great Sangarius, Ladon, Parthenius, Euenus, Ardescus, and divine Scamander.

(ll. 346-370) Also she brought forth a holy company of daughters (15) who with the lord Apollo and the Rivers have youths in their keeping -- to this charge Zeus appointed them -- Peitho, and Admete, and Ianthe, and Electra, and Doris, and Prymno, and Urania divine in form, Hippo, Clymene, Rhodea, and Callirrhoe, Zeuxo and Clytie, and Idyia, and Pasithoe, Plexaura, and Galaxaura, and lovely Dione, Melobosis and Thoe and handsome Polydora, Cerceis lovely of form, and soft eyed Pluto, Perseis, Ianeira, Acaste, Xanthe, Petraea the fair, Menestho, and Europa, Metis, and Eurynome, and Telesto saffron-clad, Chryseis and Asia and charming Calypso, Eudora, and Tyche, Amphirho, and Ocyrrhoe, and Styx who is the chiefest of them all. These are the eldest daughters that sprang from Ocean and Tethys; but there are many besides. For there are three thousand neat-ankled daughters of Ocean who are dispersed far and wide, and in every place alike serve the earth and the deep waters, children who are glorious among Goddesses. And as many other rivers are there, babbling as they flow, sons of Ocean, whom queenly Tethys bear, but their names it is hard for a mortal man to tell, but people know those by which they severally dwell.

(ll. 371-374) And Theia was subject in love to Hyperion and bear great Helios (Sun) and clear Selene (Moon) and Eos (Dawn) who shines upon all that are on earth and upon the deathless Gods who live in the wide heaven.

(ll. 375-377) And Eurybia, bright Goddess, was joined in love to Crius and bear great Astraeus, and Pallas, and Perses who also was eminent among all men in wisdom.

(ll. 378-382) And Eos bear to Astraeus the strong-hearted winds, brightening Zephyrus, and Boreas, headlong in his course, and Notus, -- a Goddess mating in love with a God. And after these Erigenia (16) bear the star Eosphorus (Dawn-bringer), and the gleaming stars with which heaven is crowned.

(ll. 383-403) And Styx the daughter of Ocean was joined to Pallas and bear Zelus (Emulation) and trim-ankled Nike (Victory) in the house. Also she brought forth Cratos (Strength) and Bia (Force), wonderful children. These have no house apart from Zeus, nor any dwelling nor path except that wherein God leads them, but they dwell always with Zeus the loud-thunderer. For so did Styx the deathless daughter of Ocean plan on that day when the Olympian Lightener called all the deathless Gods to great Olympus, and said that whosoever of the Gods would fight with him against the Titans, he would not cast him out from his rights, but each should have the office which he had before amongst the deathless Gods. And he declared that he who was without office and rights as is just. So deathless Styx came first to Olympus with her children through the wit of her dear father. And Zeus honored her, and gave her very great gifts, for her he appointed to be the great oath of the Gods, and her children to live with him always. And as he promised, so he performed fully unto them all.

But he himself mightily reigns and rules.

(ll. 404-452) Again, Phoebe came to the desired embrace of Coeus. Then the Goddess through the love of the God conceived and brought forth dark-gowned Leto, always mild, kind to men and to the deathless Gods, mild from the beginning, gentlest in all Olympus. Also she bear Asteria of happy name, whom Perses once led to his great house to be called his dear wife. And she conceived and bear Hecate whom Zeus the son of Cronos honored above all. He gave her splendid gifts, to have a share of the earth and the unfruitful sea. She received honor also in starry heaven, and is honored exceedingly by the deathless Gods. For to this day, whenever any one of men on earth offers rich sacrifices and prays for favor according to custom, he calls upon Hecate. Great honor comes full easily to him whose prayers the Goddess receives favorably, and she bestows wealth upon him; for the power surely is with her. For as many as were born of Earth and Ocean amongst all these she has her due portion. The son of Cronos did her no wrong nor took anything away of all that was her portion among the former Titan Gods: but she holds, as the division was at the first from the beginning, privilege both in earth, and in heaven, and in sea. Also, because she is an only child, the Goddess receives not less honor, but much more still, for Zeus honors her. Whom she wills she greatly aids and advances: she sits by worshipful kings in judgment, and in the assembly whom she will is distinguished among the people. And when men arm themselves for the battle that destroys men, then the Goddess is at hand to give victory and grant glory readily to whom she will. Good is she also when men contend at the games, for there too the Goddess is with them and profits them: and he who by might and strength gets the victory wins the rich prize easily with joy, and brings glory to his parents. And she is good to stand by horsemen, whom she will: and to those whose business is in the grey uncomfortable sea, and who pray to Hecate and the loud-crashing Earth-Shaker, easily the glorious Goddess gives great catch, and easily she takes it away as soon as seen, if so she will. She is good in the byre with Hermes to increase the stock. The droves of kine and wide herds of goats and flocks of fleecy sheep, if she will, she increases from a few, or makes many to be less. So, then. albeit her mother's only child (17), she is honored amongst all the deathless Gods. And the son of Cronos made her a nurse of the young who after that day saw with their eyes the light of all-seeing Dawn. So from the beginning she is a nurse of the young, and these are her honors.

(ll. 453-491) But Rhea was subject in love to Cronos and bear splendid children, Hestia (18), Demeter, and gold-shod Hera and strong Hades, pitiless in heart, who dwells under the earth, and the loud-crashing Earth-Shaker, and wise Zeus, father of Gods and men, by whose thunder the wide earth is shaken. These great Cronos swallowed as each came forth from the womb to his mother's knees with this intent, that no other of the proud sons of Heaven should hold the kingly office amongst the deathless Gods. For he learned from Earth and starry Heaven that he was destined to be overcome by his own son, strong though he was, through the contriving of great Zeus (19). Therefore he kept no blind outlook, but watched and swallowed down his children: and unceasing grief seized Rhea. But when she was about to bear Zeus, the father of Gods and men, then she besought her own dear parents, Earth and starry Heaven, to devise some plan with her that the birth of her dear child might be concealed, and that retribution might overtake great, crafty Cronos for his own father and also for the children whom he had swallowed down. And they readily heard and obeyed their dear daughter, and told her all that was destined to happen touching Cronos the king and his stout-hearted son. So they sent her to Lyetus, to the rich land of Crete, when she was ready to bear great Zeus, the youngest of her children. Him did vast Earth receive from Rhea in wide Crete to nourish and to bring up. Thither came Earth carrying him swiftly through the black night to Lyctus first, and took him in her arms and hid him in a remote cave beneath the secret places of the holy earth on thick-wooded Mount Aegeum; but to the mightily ruling son of Heaven, the earlier king of the Gods, she gave a great stone wrapped in swaddling clothes. Then he took it in his hands and thrust it down into his belly: wretch! he knew not in his heart that in place of the stone his son was left behind, unconquered and untroubled, and that he was soon to overcome him by force and might and drive him from his honors, himself to reign over the deathless Gods.

(ll. 492-506) After that, the strength and glorious limbs of the prince increased quickly, and as the years rolled on, great Cronos the wily was beguiled by the deep suggestions of Earth, and brought up again his offspring, vanquished by the arts and might of his own son, and he vomited up first the stone which he had swallowed last. And Zeus set it fast in the wide-pathed earth at goodly Pytho under the glens of Parnassus, to be a sign thenceforth and a marvel to mortal men (20). And he set free from their deadly bonds the brothers of his father, sons of Heaven whom his father in his foolishness had bound. And they remembered to be grateful to him for his kindness, and gave him thunder and the glowing thunderbolt and lightening: for before that, huge Earth had hidden these. In them he trusts and rules over mortals and immortals.

(ll. 507-543) Now Iapetus took to wife the neat-ankled mad Clymene, daughter of Ocean, and went up with her into one bed. And she bear him a stout-hearted son, Atlas: also she bear very glorious Menoetius and clever Prometheus, full of various wiles, and scatter-brained Epimetheus who from the first was a mischief to men who eat bread; for it was he who first took of Zeus the woman, the maiden whom he had formed. But Menoetius was outrageous, and far-seeing Zeus struck him with a lurid thunderbolt and sent him down to Erebus because of his mad presumption and exceeding pride. And Atlas through hard constraint upholds the wide heaven with unwearying head and arms, standing at the borders of the earth before the clear-voiced Hesperides; for this lot wise Zeus assigned to him. And ready-witted Prometheus he bound with inextricable bonds, cruel chains, and drove a shaft through his middle, and set on him a long-winged eagle, which used to eat his immortal liver; but by night the liver grew as much again everyway as the long-winged bird devoured in the whole day. That bird Heracles, the valiant son of shapely-ankled Alcmene, slew; and delivered the son of Iapetus from the cruel plague, and released him from his affliction -- not without the will of Olympian Zeus who reigns on high, that the glory of Heracles the Theban-born might be yet greater than it was before over the plenteous earth. This, then, he regarded, and honored his famous son; though he was angry, he ceased from the wrath which he had before because Prometheus matched himself in wit with the almighty son of Cronos. For when the Gods and mortal men had a dispute at Mecone, even then Prometheus was forward to cut up a great ox and set portions before them, trying to befool the mind of Zeus. Before the rest he set flesh and inner parts thick with fat upon the hide, covering them with an ox paunch; but for Zeus he put the white bones dressed up with cunning art and covered with shining fat. Then the father of men and of Gods said to him:

(ll. 543-544) 'Son of Iapetus, most glorious of all lords, good sir, how unfairly you have divided the portions!'

(ll. 545-547) So said Zeus whose wisdom is everlasting, rebuking him. But wily Prometheus answered him, smiling softly and not forgetting his cunning trick:

(ll. 548-558) 'Zeus, most glorious and greatest of the eternal Gods, take which ever of these portions your heart within you bids.' So he said, thinking trickery. But Zeus, whose wisdom is everlasting, saw and failed not to perceive the trick, and in his heart he thought mischief against mortal men which also was to be fulfilled. With both hands he took up the white fat and was angry at heart, and wrath came to his spirit when he saw the white ox-bones craftily tricked out: and because of this the tribes of men upon earth burn white bones to the deathless Gods upon fragrant altars. But Zeus who drives the clouds was greatly vexed and said to him:

(ll. 559-560) 'Son of Iapetus, clever above all! So, sir, you have not yet forgotten your cunning arts!'

(ll. 561-584) So spoke Zeus in anger, whose wisdom is everlasting; and from that time he was always mindful of the trick, and would not give the power of unwearying fire to the Melian (21) race of mortal men who live on the earth. But the noble son of Iapetus outwitted him and stole the far-seen gleam of unwearying fire in a hollow fennel stalk. And Zeus who thunders on high was stung in spirit, and his dear heart was angered when he saw amongst men the far-seen ray of fire. Forthwith he made an evil thing for men as the price of fire; for the very famous Limping God formed of earth the likeness of a shy maiden as the son of Cronos willed. And the Goddess bright-eyed Athena girded and clothed her with silvery raiment, and down from her head she spread with her hands a broidered veil, a wonder to see; and she, Pallas Athena, put about her head lovely garlands, flowers of new-grown herbs. Also she put upon her head a crown of gold which the very famous Limping God made himself and worked with his own hands as a favor to Zeus his father. On it was much curious work, wonderful to see; for of the many creatures which the land and sea rear up, he put most upon it, wonderful things, like living beings with voices: and great beauty shone out from it.

(ll. 585-589) But when he had made the beautiful evil to be the price for the blessing, he brought her out, delighting in the finery which the bright-eyed daughter of a mighty father had given her, to the place where the other Gods and men were. And wonder took hold of the deathless Gods and mortal men when they saw that which was sheer guile, not to be withstood by men.

(ll. 590-612) For from her is the race of women and female kind: of her is the deadly race and tribe of women who live amongst mortal men to their great trouble, no helpmeets in hateful poverty, but only in wealth. And as in thatched hives bees feed the drones whose nature is to do mischief -- by day and throughout the day until the sun goes down the bees are busy and lay the white combs, while the drones stay at home in the covered skeps and reap the toil of others into their own bellies -- even so Zeus who thunders on high made women to be an evil to mortal men, with a nature to do evil. And he gave them a second evil to be the price for the good they had: whoever avoids marriage and the sorrows that women cause, and will not wed, reaches deadly old age without anyone to tend his years, and though he at least has no lack of livelihood while he lives, yet, when he is dead, his kinsfolk divide his possessions amongst them. And as for the man who chooses the lot of marriage and takes a good wife suited to his mind, evil continually contends with good; for whoever happens to have mischievous children, lives always with unceasing grief in his spirit and heart within him; and this evil cannot be healed.

(ll. 613-616) So it is not possible to deceive or go beyond the will of Zeus; for not even the son of Iapetus, kindly Prometheus, escaped his heavy anger, but of necessity strong bands confined him, although he knew many a wile.

(ll. 617-643) But when first their father was vexed in his heart with Obriareus and Cottus and Gyes, he bound them in cruel bonds, because he was jealous of their exceeding manhood and comeliness and great size: and he made them live beneath the wide-pathed earth, where they were afflicted, being set to dwell under the ground, at the end of the earth, at its great borders, in bitter anguish for a long time and with great grief at heart. But the son of Cronos and the other deathless Gods whom rich-haired Rhea bear from union with Cronos, brought them up again to the light at Earth's advising. For she herself recounted all things to the Gods fully, how that with these they would gain victory and a glorious cause to vaunt themselves. For the Titan Gods and as many as sprang from Cronos had long been fighting together in stubborn war with heart-grieving toil, the lordly Titans from high Othyrs, but the Gods, givers of good, whom rich-haired Rhea bear in union with Cronos, from Olympus. So they, with bitter wrath, were fighting continually with one another at that time for ten full years, and the hard strife had no close or end for either side, and the issue of the war hung evenly balanced. But when he had provided those three with all things fitting, nectar and ambrosia which the Gods themselves eat, and when their proud spirit revived within them all after they had fed on nectar and delicious ambrosia, and then it was that the father of men and Gods spoke amongst them:

(ll. 644-653) 'Hear me, bright children of Earth and Heaven, that I may say what my heart within me bids. A long while now have we, who are sprung from Cronos and the Titan Gods, fought with each other every day to get victory and to prevail. But do you show your great might and unconquerable strength, and face the Titans in bitter strife; for remember our friendly kindness, and from what sufferings you are come back to the light from your cruel bondage under misty gloom through our counsels.'

(ll. 654-663) So he said. And blameless Cottus answered him again: 'Divine one, you speak that which we know well: nay, even of ourselves we know that your wisdom and understanding is exceeding, and that you became a defender of the deathless ones from chill doom. And through your devising we are come back again from the murky gloom and from our merciless bonds, enjoying what we looked not for, O lord, son of Cronos. And so now with fixed purpose and deliberate counsel we will aid your power in dreadful strife and will fight against the Titans in hard battle.'

(ll. 664-686) So he said: and the Gods, givers of good things, applauded when they heard his word, and their spirit longed for war even more than before, and they all, both male and female, stirred up hated battle that day, the Titan Gods, and all that were born of Cronos together with those dread, mighty ones of overwhelming strength whom Zeus brought up to the light from Erebus beneath the earth. An hundred arms sprang from the shoulders of all alike, and each had fifty heads growing upon his shoulders upon stout limbs. These, then, stood against the Titans in grim strife, holding huge rocks in their strong hands. And on the other part the Titans eagerly strengthened their ranks, and both sides at one time showed the work of their hands and their might. The boundless sea rang terribly around, and the earth crashed loudly: wide Heaven was shaken and groaned, and high Olympus reeled from its foundation under the charge of the undying Gods, and a heavy quaking reached dim Tartarus and the deep sound of their feet in the fearful onset and of their hard missiles. So, then, they launched their grievous shafts upon one another, and the cry of both armies as they shouted reached to starry heaven; and they met together with a great battle-cry.

(ll. 687-712) Then Zeus no longer held back his might; but straight his heart was filled with fury and he showed forth all his strength. From Heaven and from Olympus he came forthwith, hurling his lightning: the bold flew thick and fast from his strong hand together with thunder and lightning, whirling an awesome flame. The life-giving earth crashed around in burning, and the vast wood crackled loud with fire all about. All the land seethed, and Ocean's streams and the unfruitful sea. The hot vapor lapped round the earthborn Titans: flame unspeakable rose to the bright upper air: the flashing glare of the thunder- stone and lightning blinded their eyes for all that there were strong. Astounding heat seized Chaos: and to see with eyes and to hear the sound with ears it seemed even as if Earth and wide Heaven above came together; for such a mighty crash would have arisen if Earth were being hurled to ruin, and Heaven from on high were hurling her down; so great a crash was there while the Gods were meeting together in strife. Also the winds brought rumbling earthquake and dust storm, thunder and lightning and the lurid thunderbolt, which are the shafts of great Zeus, and carried the clangor and the war-cry into the midst of the two hosts. A horrible uproar of terrible strife arose: mighty deeds were shown and the battle inclined. But until then, they kept at one another and fought continually in cruel war.

(ll. 713-735) And amongst the foremost Cottus and Briareos and Gyes insatiate for war raised fierce fighting: three hundred rocks, one upon another, they launched from their strong hands and overshadowed the Titans with their missiles, and buried them beneath the wide-pathed earth, and bound them in bitter chains when they had conquered them by their strength for all their great spirit, as far beneath the earth to Tartarus. For a brazen anvil falling down from heaven nine nights and days would reach the earth upon the tenth: and again, a brazen anvil falling from earth nine nights and days would reach Tartarus upon the tenth. Round it runs a fence of bronze, and night spreads in triple line all about it like a neck-circlet, while above grow the roots of the earth and unfruitful sea. There by the counsel of Zeus who drives the clouds the Titan Gods are hidden under misty gloom, in a dank place where are the ends of the huge earth. And they may not go out; for Poseidon fixed gates of bronze upon it, and a wall runs all round it on every side. There Gyes and Cottus and great-souled Obriareus live, trusty warders of Zeus who holds the aegis.

(ll. 736-744) And there, all in their order, are the sources and ends of gloomy earth and misty Tartarus and the unfruitful sea and starry heaven, loathsome and dank, which even the Gods abhor.

It is a great gulf, and if once a man were within the gates, he would not reach the floor until a whole year had reached its end, but cruel blast upon blast would carry him this way and that. And this marvel is awful even to the deathless Gods.

(ll. 744-757) There stands the awful home of murky Night wrapped in dark clouds. In front of it the son of Iapetus (22) stands immovably upholding the wide heaven upon his head and unwearying hands, where Night and Day draw near and greet one another as they pass the great threshold of bronze: and while the one is about to go down into the house, the other comes out at the door.

And the house never holds them both within; but always one is without the house passing over the earth, while the other stays at home and waits until the time for her journeying come; and the one holds all-seeing light for them on earth, but the other holds in her arms Sleep the brother of Death, even evil Night, wrapped in a vaporous cloud.

(ll. 758-766) And there the children of dark Night have their dwellings, Sleep and Death, awful Gods. The glowing Sun never looks upon them with his beams, neither as he goes up into heaven, nor as he comes down from heaven. And the former of them roams peacefully over the earth and the sea's broad back and is kindly to men; but the other has a heart of iron, and his spirit within him is pitiless as bronze: whomsoever of men he has once seized he holds fast: and he is hateful even to the deathless Gods.

(ll. 767-774) There, in front, stand the echoing halls of the God of the lower-world, strong Hades, and of awful Persephone. A fearful hound guards the house in front, pitiless, and he has a cruel trick. On those who go in he fawns with his tail and both is ears, but suffers them not to go out back again, but keeps watch and devours whomsoever he catches going out of the gates of strong Hades and awful Persephone.

(ll. 775-806) And there dwells the Goddess loathed by the deathless Gods, terrible Styx, eldest daughter of back-flowing (23) Ocean. She lives apart from the Gods in her glorious house vaulted over with great rocks and propped up to heaven all round with silver pillars. Rarely does the daughter of Thaumas, swift- footed Iris, come to her with a message over the sea's wide back.

But when strife and quarrel arise among the deathless Gods, and when any of them who live in the house of Olympus lies, then Zeus sends Iris to bring in a golden jug the great oath of the Gods from far away, the famous cold water which trickles down from a high and beetling rock. Far under the wide-pathed earth a branch of Oceanus flows through the dark night out of the holy stream, and a tenth part of his water is allotted to her. With nine silver-swirling streams he winds about the earth and the sea's wide back, and then falls into the main (24); but the tenth flows out from a rock, a sore trouble to the Gods. For whoever of the deathless Gods that hold the peaks of snowy Olympus pours a libation of her water is forsworn, lies breathless until a full year is completed, and never comes near to taste ambrosia and nectar, but lies spiritless and voiceless on a strewn bed: and a heavy trance overshadows him. But when he has spent a long year in his sickness, another penance and a harder follows after the first. For nine years he is cut off from the eternal Gods and never joins their councils of their feasts, nine full years. But in the tenth year he comes again to join the assemblies of the deathless Gods who live in the house of Olympus. Such an oath, then, did the Gods appoint the eternal and primeval water of Styx to be: and it spouts through a rugged place.

(ll. 807-819) And there, all in their order, are the sources and ends of the dark earth and misty Tartarus and the unfruitful sea and starry heaven, loathsome and dank, which even the Gods abhor.

And there are shining gates and an immoveable threshold of bronze having unending roots and it is grown of itself (25). And beyond, away from all the Gods, live the Titans, beyond gloomy Chaos. But the glorious allies of loud-crashing Zeus have their dwelling upon Ocean's foundations, even Cottus and Gyes; but Briareos, being goodly, the deep-roaring Earth-Shaker made his son-in-law, giving him Cymopolea his daughter to wed.

(ll. 820-868) But when Zeus had driven the Titans from heaven, huge Earth bear her youngest child Typhoeus of the love of Tartarus, by the aid of golden Aphrodite. Strength was with his hands in all that he did and the feet of the strong God were untiring. From his shoulders grew an hundred heads of a snake, a fearful dragon, with dark, flickering tongues, and from under the brows of his eyes in his marvelous heads flashed fire, and fire burned from his heads as he glared. And there were voices in all his dreadful heads which uttered every kind of sound unspeakable; for at one time they made sounds such that the Gods understood, but at another, the noise of a bull bellowing aloud in proud ungovernable fury; and at another, the sound of a lion, relentless of heart; and at another's, sounds like whelps, wonderful to hear; and again, at another, he would hiss, so that the high mountains re-echoed. And truly a thing past help would have happened on that day, and he would have come to reign over mortals and immortals, had not the father of men and Gods been quick to perceive it. But he thundered hard and mightily: and the earth around resounded terribly and the wide heaven above, and the sea and Ocean's streams and the nether parts of the earth. Great Olympus reeled beneath the divine feet of the king as he arose and earth groaned thereat. And through the two of them heat took hold on the dark-blue sea, through the thunder and lightning, and through the fire from the monster, and the scorching winds and blazing thunderbolt. The whole earth seethed, and sky and sea: and the long waves raged along the beaches round and about, at the rush of the deathless Gods: and there arose an endless shaking. Hades trembled where he rules over the dead below, and the Titans under Tartarus who live with Cronos, because of the unending clamor and the fearful strife. So when Zeus had rose up his might and seized his arms, thunder and lightning and lurid thunderbolt, he leaped form Olympus and struck him, and burned all the marvelous heads of the monster about him. But when Zeus had conquered him and lashed him with strokes, Typhoeus was hurled down, a maimed wreck, so that the huge earth groaned. And flame shot forth from the thunder- stricken lord in the dim rugged glens of the mount (26), when he was smitten. A great part of huge earth was scorched by the terrible vapor and melted as tin melts when heated by men's art in channeled (27) crucibles; or as iron, which is hardest of all things, is softened by glowing fire in mountain glens and melts in the divine earth through the strength of Hephaestus (28). Even so, then, the earth melted in the glow of the blazing fire. And in the bitterness of his anger Zeus cast him into wide Tartarus.

(ll. 869-880) And from Typhoeus come boisterous winds which blow damply, except Notus and Boreas and clear Zephyr. These are a God-sent kind, and a great blessing to men; but the others blow fitfully upon the seas. Some rush upon the misty sea and work great havoc among men with their evil, raging blasts; for varying with the season they blow, scattering ships and destroying sailors. And men who meet these upon the sea have no help against the mischief. Others again over the boundless, flowering earth spoil the fair fields of men who dwell below, filling them with dust and cruel uproar.

(ll. 881-885) But when the blessed Gods had finished their toil, and settled by force their struggle for honors with the Titans, they pressed far-seeing Olympian Zeus to reign and to rule over them, by Earth's prompting. So he divided their dignities amongst them.

(ll. 886-900) Now Zeus, king of the Gods, made Metis his wife first, and she was wisest among Gods and mortal men. But when she was about to bring forth the Goddess bright-eyed Athena, Zeus craftily deceived her with cunning words and put her in his own belly, as Earth and starry Heaven advised. For they advised him so, to the end that no other should hold royal sway over the eternal Gods in place of Zeus; for very wise children were destined to be born of her, first the maiden bright-eyed Tritogeneia, equal to her father in strength and in wise understanding; but afterwards she was to bear a son of overbearing spirit, king of Gods and men. But Zeus put her into his own belly first, that the Goddess might devise for him both good and evil.

(ll. 901-906) Next he married bright Themis who bear the Horae (Hours), and Eunomia (Order), Dike (Justice), and blooming Eirene (Peace), who mind the works of mortal men, and the Moerae (Fates) to whom wise Zeus gave the greatest honor, Clotho, and Lachesis, and Atropos who give mortal men evil and good to have.

(ll. 907-911) And Eurynome, the daughter of Ocean, beautiful in form, bear him three fair-cheeked Charites (Graces), Aglaea, and Euphrosyne, and lovely Thaleia, from whose eyes as they glanced flowed love that unnerves the limbs: and beautiful is their glance beneath their brows.

(ll. 912-914) Also he came to the bed of all-nourishing Demeter, and she bear white-armed Persephone whom Aidoneus carried off from her mother; but wise Zeus gave her to him.

(ll. 915-917) And again, he loved Mnemosyne with the beautiful hair: and of her the nine gold-crowned Muses were born who delight in feasts and the pleasures of song.

(ll. 918-920) And Leto was joined in love with Zeus who holds the aegis, and bear Apollo and Artemis delighting in arrows, children lovely above all the sons of Heaven.

(ll. 921-923) Lastly, he made Hera his blooming wife: and she was joined in love with the king of Gods and men, and brought forth Hebe and Ares and Eileithyia.

(ll. 924-929) But Zeus himself gave birth from his own head to bright-eyed Tritogeneia (29), the awful, the strife-stirring, the host-leader, the unwearying, the queen, who delights in tumults and wars and battles. But Hera without union with Zeus -- for she was very angry and quarreled with her mate -- bear famous Hephaestus, who is skilled in crafts more than all the sons of Heaven.

(ll. 929a-929t) (30) But Hera was very angry and quarreled with her mate. And because of this strife she bear without union with Zeus who holds the aegis a glorious son, Hephaestus, who excelled all the sons of Heaven in crafts. But Zeus lay with the fair- cheeked daughter of Ocean and Tethys apart from Hera.... ((LACUNA)) ....deceiving Metis (Thought) although she was full wise. But he seized her with his hands and put her in his belly, for fear that she might bring forth something stronger than his thunderbolt: therefore did Zeus, who sits on high and dwells in the ether, swallow her down suddenly. But she straightway conceived Pallas Athena: and the father of men and Gods gave her birth by way of his head on the banks of the river Trito. And she remained hidden beneath the inward parts of Zeus, even Metis, Athena's mother, worker of righteousness, who was wiser than Gods and mortal men. There the Goddess (Athena) received that (31) whereby she excelled in strength all the deathless ones who dwell in Olympus, she who made the host-scaring weapon of Athena. And with it (Zeus) gave her birth, arrayed in arms of war.

(ll. 930-933) And of Amphitrite and the loud-roaring Earth-Shaker was born great, wide-ruling Triton, and he owns the depths of the sea, living with his dear mother and the lord his father in their golden house, an awful God.

(ll. 933-937) Also Cytherea bear to Ares the shield-piercer Panic and Fear, terrible Gods who drive in disorder the close ranks of men in numbing war, with the help of Ares, sacker of towns: and Harmonia whom high-spirited Cadmus made his wife.

(ll. 938-939) And Maia, the daughter of Atlas, bear to Zeus glorious Hermes, the herald of the deathless Gods, for she went up into his holy bed.

(ll. 940-942) And Semele, daughter of Cadmus was joined with him in love and bear him a splendid son, joyous Dionysus, -- a mortal woman an immortal son. And now they both are Gods.

(ll. 943-944) And Alemena was joined in love with Zeus who drives the clouds and bear mighty Heracles.

(ll. 945-946) And Hephaestus, the famous Lame One, made Aglaea, youngest of the Graces, his buxom wife.

(ll. 947-949) And golden-haired Dionysus made brown-haired Ariadne, the daughter of Minos, his buxom wife: and the son of Cronos made her deathless and unaging for him.

(ll. 950-955) And mighty Heracles, the valiant son of neat-ankled Alemena, when he had finished his grievous toils, made Hebe the child of great Zeus and gold-shod Hera his shy wife in snowy Olympus. Happy he! For he has finished his great works and lives amongst the dying Gods, untroubled and unaging all his days.

(ll. 956-962) And Perseis, the daughter of Ocean, bear to unwearying Helios Circe and Aeetes the king. And Aeetes, the son of Helios who shows light to men, took to wife fair-cheeked Idyia, daughter of Ocean the perfect stream, by the will of the Gods: and she was subject to him in love through golden Aphrodite and bear him neat-ankled Medea.

(ll. 963-968) And now farewell, you dwellers on Olympus and you islands and continents and thou briny sea within. Now sing the company of Goddesses, sweet-voiced Muses of Olympus, daughter of Zeus who holds the aegis, -- even those deathless one who lay with mortal men and bear children like unto Gods.

(ll. 969-974) Demeter, bright Goddess, was joined in sweet love with the Hero Iasion in a thrice-ploughed fallow in the rich land of Crete, and bear Plutus, a kindly God who goes everywhere over land and the sea's wide back, and him who finds him and into whose hands he comes he makes rich, bestowing great wealth upon him.

(ll. 975-978) And Harmonia, the daughter of golden Aphrodite, bear to Cadmus Ino and Semele and fair-cheeked Agave and Autonoe whom long haired Aristaeus wedded, and Polydorus also in rich- crowned Thebe.

(ll. 979-983) And the daughter of Ocean, Callirrhoe was joined in the love of rich Aphrodite with stout hearted Chrysaor and bears a son who was the strongest of all men, Geryones, whom mighty Heracles killed in sea-girt Erythea for the sake of his shambling oxen.

(ll. 984-991) And Eos bear to Tithonus brazen-crested Memnon, king of the Ethiopians, and the Lord Emathion. And to Cephalus she bear a splendid son, strong Phaethon, a man like the Gods, whom, when he was a young boy in the tender flower of glorious youth with childish thoughts, laughter-loving Aphrodite seized and caught up and made a keeper of her shrine by night, a divine spirit.

(ll. 993-1002) And the son of Aeson by the will of the Gods led away from Aeetes the daughter of Aeetes the heaven-nurtured king, when he had finished the many grievous labors which the great king, over bearing Pelias, that outrageous and presumptuous doer of violence, put upon him. But when the son of Aeson had finished them, he came to Iolcus after long toil bringing the coy-eyed girl with him on his swift ship, and made her his buxom wife. And she was subject to Iason, shepherd of the people, and bear a son Medeus whom Cheiron the son of Philyra brought up in the mountains. And the will of great Zeus was fulfilled.

(ll. 1003-1007) But of the daughters of Nereus, the Old man of the Sea, Psamathe the fair Goddess, was loved by Aeacus through golden Aphrodite and bear Phocus. And the silver-shod Goddess Thetis was subject to Peleus and brought forth lion-hearted Achilles, the destroyer of men.

(ll. 1008-1010) And Cytherea with the beautiful crown was joined in sweet love with the Hero Anchises and bear Aeneas on the peaks of Ida with its many wooded glens.

(ll. 1011-1016) And Circe the daughter of Helios, Hyperion's son, loved steadfast Odysseus and bear Agrius and Latinus who was faultless and strong: also she brought forth Telegonus by the will of golden Aphrodite. And they ruled over the famous Tyrenians, very far off in a recess of the holy islands.

(ll. 1017-1018) And the bright Goddess Calypso was joined to Odysseus in sweet love, and bear him Nausithous and Nausinous.

(ll. 1019-1020) These are the immortal Goddesses who lay with mortal men and bear them children like unto Gods.

(ll. 1021-1022) But now, sweet-voiced Muses of Olympus, daughters of Zeus who holds the aegis, sing of the company of women.

ENDNOTES:

(1) The epithet probably indicates coquettishness.

(2) A proverbial saying meaning, 'why enlarge on irrelevant topics?'

(3) 'She of the noble voice': Calliope is queen of Epic poetry.

(4) Earth, in the cosmology of Hesiod, is a disk surrounded by the river Oceanus and floating upon a waste of waters. It is called the foundation of all (the qualification 'the deathless ones...' etc. is an interpolation), because not only trees, men, and animals, but even the hills and seas (ll. 129, 131) are supported by it.

(5) Ether is the bright, untainted upper atmosphere, as distinguished from Air, the lower atmosphere of the earth.

(6) Brontes is the Thunderer; Steropes, the Lightener; and Arges, the Vivid One.

(7) The myth accounts for the separation of Heaven and Earth. In Egyptian cosmology Nut (the Sky) is thrust and held apart from her brother Geb (the Earth) by their father Shu, who corresponds to the Greek Atlas.

(8) Nymphs of the ash-trees, as Dryads are nymphs of the oak- trees. Cp. note on "Works and Days", l. 145.

(9) 'Member-loving': the title is perhaps only a perversion of the regular PHILOMEIDES (laughter-loving).

(10) Cletho (the Spinner) is she who spins the thread of man's life; Lachesis (the Disposer of Lots) assigns to each man his destiny; Atropos (She who cannot be turned) is the 'Fury with the abhorred shears.'

(11) Many of the names which follow express various qualities or aspects of the sea: thus Galene is 'Calm', Cymothoe is the 'Wave-swift', Pherusa and Dynamene are 'She who speeds (ships)' and 'She who has power'.

(12) The 'Wave-receiver' and the 'Wave-stiller'.

(13) 'The Unerring' or 'Truthful'; cp. l. 235.

(14) i.e. Poseidon.

(15) Goettling notes that some of these nymphs derive their names from lands over which they preside, as Europa, Asia, Doris, Ianeira ('Lady of the Ionians'), but that most are called after some quality which their streams possessed: thus Xanthe is the 'Brown' or 'Turbid', Amphirho is the 'Surrounding' river, Ianthe is 'She who delights', and Ocyrrhoe is the 'Swift-flowing'.

(16) i.e. Eos, the 'Early-born'.

(17) Van Lennep explains that Hecate, having no brothers to support her claim, might have been slighted.

(18) The Goddess of the hearth (the Roman "Vesta"), and so of the

house. Cp. "Homeric Hymns" v.22 ff.; xxxix.1 ff.

(19) The variant reading 'of his father' (sc. Heaven) rests on inferior MS. authority and is probably an alteration due to the difficulty stated by a Scholiast: 'How could Zeus, being not yet begotten, plot against his father?' The phrase is, however, part of the prophecy. The whole line may well be spurious, and is rejected by Heyne, Wolf, Gaisford and Guyet.

(20) Pausanias (x. 24.6) saw near the tomb of Neoptolemus 'a stone of no great size', which the Delphians anointed every day with oil, and which he says was supposed to be the stone given to Cronos.

(21) A Scholiast explains: 'Either because they (men) sprang from the Melian nymphs (cp. l. 187); or because, when they were born (?), they cast themselves under the ash-trees, that is, the trees.' The reference may be to the origin of men from ash-trees: cp. "Works and Days", l. 145 and note.

(22) sc. Atlas, the Shu of Egyptian mythology: cp. note on line 177.

(23) Oceanus is here regarded as a continuous stream enclosing the earth and the seas, and so as flowing back upon himself.

(24) The conception of Oceanus is here different: he has nine streams which encircle the earth and the flow out into the 'main' which appears to be the waste of waters on which, according to early Greek and Hebrew cosmology, the disk-like earth floated.

(25) i.e. the threshold is of 'native' metal, and not artificial.

(26) According to Homer Typhoeus was overwhelmed by Zeus amongst the Arimi in Cilicia. Pindar represents him as buried under Aetna, and Tzetzes reads Aetna in this passage.

(27) The epithet (which means literally 'well-bored') seems to refer to the spout of the crucible.

(28) The fire God. There is no reference to volcanic action: iron was smelted on Mount Ida; cp. "Epigrams of Homer", ix. 2-4.

(29) i.e. Athena, who was born 'on the banks of the river Trito' (cp. l. 929l)

(30) Restored by Peppmuller. The nineteen following lines from another recession of lines 889-900, 924-9 are quoted by Chrysippus (in Galen).

(31) sc. the aegis. Line 929s is probably spurious, since it disagrees with l. 929q and contains a suspicious reference to Athens.

Appendix III:
The Emperor Julian's Oration to the Sovereign Sun
translated by Taylor Thomas (1793)
edited by Timothy Jay Alexander

IT APPEARS TO me that the present oration very properly belongs to all

> --who breathe or creep on earth,

who participate of being, of a rational soul, and of intellect; but I consider it as particularly belonging to myself; for I am an attendant of the sovereign Sun: and of the truth of this, indeed, I possess most accurate assurances, one of which it may be lawful for me, without envy, to relate. A vehement love for the splendors of this God took possession of me from my youth; in consequence of which, while I was a boy, my rational part was ravished with astonishment as often as I surveyed his ethereal light; nor was I alone desirous of steadfastly beholding his diurnal splendors, but likewise at night, when the heavens were clear and serene, I was accustomed to walk abroad, and, neglecting every other concern, to gaze on the beauty of the celestial regions with rapturous delight: indeed I was so lost in attentive vision, that I was equally unconscious of another's discourse, and of my own conduct on such occasions. Hence I appeared to be too studious of their contemplation, and too curious in such employments; and, in consequence of this, though I was yet short of the perfection of manhood, I was suspected by some to be skilled in astronomical divination; but, indeed, no book of this kind was as yet in my possession, and I was entirely ignorant of its meaning and use. But why do I relate such trifling particulars, when I have things of far greater moment to declare, if I should tell my conceptions of the Gods at that period of life. However, let the darkness of childhood be consigned to the shades of oblivion. But that the celestial light, with which I was every way environed, so excited and exalted me to its contemplation, that I observed by myself the contrary course of the moon to that of the universe, before I met with any who philosophized on these subjects, may easily be credited from the indications which I have previously related. Indeed I admire the felicity of the man on whom divinity bestows a body united from sacred and prophetic seed, that he may disclose the treasuries of wisdom; but, at the same time, I will not despise the condition allotted me by the benefit of this deity; I mean, that I rank among those to whom the dominion and empire of the earth at the present period belong.

It is, indeed, my opinion, that the sun (if we may credit the wise) is the common father of all mankind; for as it is very properly said, man and the sun generate man. But this deity disseminates souls into the earth not from himself alone, but from other divinities; and these evince by their lives the end of their propagation. And his destiny will indeed be most illustrious, who, prior to his third progeny, and from a long series of ancestors, has been addicted to the service of this deity: nor is this to be despised, if some one, knowing himself to be naturally a servant of this God, alone among all, or with a few of mankind, delivers himself to the cultivation of his lord.

Let us then, to the best of our ability, celebrate his festival, which the royal city renders illustrious by its annual sacrifices and solemn rites. But I am well aware how difficult it is to conceive the nature of the unapparent sun, if we may conjecture from the excellence of the apparent God; and to declare this to others, can perhaps be accomplished by no one without derogating from the dignity of the subject; for I am fully convinced that no one can attain to, the dignity of his nature: however, to possess a mediocrity in celebrating his majesty, appears to be the summit of human attainments. But may Mercury, the ruling deity of discourse, together with the Muses, and their leader, Apollo, be present in this undertaking; for this oration pertains to Apollo; and may they enable me so to speak of the immortal Gods, that the credibility of my narration may be grateful and acceptable to their divinities. What mode of celebration then shall we adopt? Shall we, if we speak of his nature and origin, of his power and energies, as well manifest as occult, and besides this, of the communication of good which he largely distributes to every world, shall we, I say, by this means, frame an encomium, not perfectly abhorrent from the God? Let us therefore begin our oration from hence.

That divine and all-beautiful world, then, which, from the supreme arch of the heavens, to the extremity of the earth, is contained by the immutable providence of the deity, existed from eternity without any generation, and will be eternal through all the following periods of time; nor is it guarded by any other substance, than by the proximate investiture of the fifth body, the summit of which is the solar ray, situated, as it were, in the second degree from the intelligible world: but it is more anciently comprehended by the king and moderator of all things, about whom the universe subsists. This cause therefore, whether it is lawful to call him that which is superior to intellect; or the idea of the things which are, (but whom I should call the intelligible whole;) or the One, since the One appears to be the most ancient of all things; or that which Plato is accustomed to denominate the Good; this uniform cause, then, of the universe, who is to all beings the. administrator of beauty, perfection, union, and immeasurable power, according to a primary nature abiding in himself, produced from himself as a medium between the middle intellectual and demiurgic causes, that mighty divinity the sun perfectly similar to himself. And this was the opinion of the divine Plato, when he says: "This is what I called the son of the Good, which the Good generated analogous to itself: that as this in the intelligible place is to intellect and the objects of intelligence, so is that in the visible place to sight and the objects of sight." Hence it appears to me, that light has the same proportion to that which is visible, as truth to that which is intelligible, But this intelligible universe, as it, is the progeny of the idea of the first and greatest good, eternally abiding about his stable essence, obtains the supremacy among the intellectual Gods; and is the, source of the same perfection to these, as the Good to the intelligible Gods. But according to my opinion, good is to intelligibles the cause of beauty, essence, perfection, and union; comprehending and illuminating their nature by its boniform power: the sun therefore distributes the same excellences to the intellectual Gods, of whom he is appointed the sovereign ruler by the ordination of the Good. At the same time, it must be observed, that these. Gods are coexistent with this intellectual sun; by means of which, as it appears to me, from exerting a boniform cause among the intellectual Gods, he administers all things according to the invariable rectitude of intellect.

But besides this, the third divine principle, I mean the apparent and splendid orbicular sun, is the cause of well-being to sensible natures; and whatever we have asserted as flowing from the mighty intellectual sun among the intellectual Gods, the same perfections the apparent sun communicates to apparent forms; and the truth of this will be clearly evinced by contemplating invisible natures, from the objects of sensible inspection. Let us then begin the contemplation. And, in the first place, is not light the incorporeal and divine form of that which is diaphanous in energy? But whatever that which is diaphanous may be, which is subjected to all the elements, and is their proximate form, it is certain that it is neither corporeal nor mixed, nor does it display any of the peculiar qualities of body. Hence you cannot affirm that heat is one of its properties, nor its contrary cold; you can neither ascribe to it hardness nor softness, nor any other tangible difference; nor attribute taste or smell as peculiarities of its essence: for a nature of this kind, which is called forth into energy by the interposition of light, is alone subject to the power of sight. But light is the form of a diaphanous essence, which resembles that common matter, the subject of bodies, through which it is every where diffused; and rays are the summit, and as it were, flower of light, which is an incorporeal nature. But according to the opinion of the Phoenicians, who are skilled in divine science and wisdom, the universally-diffused splendor of light is the sincere energy of an intellect perfectly pure; and this doctrine will be found agreeable to reason, when we consider, that since light is incorporeal, its fountain cannot be body, but the sincere energy of intellect, illuminating in its proper habitation the middle region of the heavens: and from this exalted situation scattering its light, it fills all the celestial orbs with powerful vigor, and illuminates the universe with divine and incorruptible light.

But the operations of this pure intellect on the Gods we have already briefly exhibited, and we shall shortly more largely discuss; for whatever we first perceive by the sight, is nothing but a mere name of honorable labor, unless it receives the ruling assistance of light: for how can any thing be visible unless, like matter, it is moved to the artificer that it may receive the supervening investments of form? Just as gold in a state of simple fusion is indeed gold, but is not a statue or an image till the artificer invests it with form: in a similar manner all naturally visible objects cease to be apparent unless light is present with the perceiver. Hence, since it confers vision on the perceiver, and visibility on the objects of perception, it perfects two natures in energy, sight and that which is visible; but perfections are form and essence; though perhaps an assertion of this kind is more subtle than is suited to our present purpose. However, of this all men are persuaded, both the scientific and the illiterate, philosophers and the learned, that day and night are fabricated by the power of this rising and setting divinity; and that he manifestly changes and convolves the world. But to which of the other stars does a province of this kind belong? Do we not therefore derive conviction from hence, that the unapparent and divine race of intellectual Gods, above the heavens, are replenished from the sun with conform powers; to whose authority the whole choir of the stars submits; and whose nod generation, which he governs by his providence, attentively obeys? For the planets, indeed, dancing round him as their king, harmoniously revolve in a circle, with definite intervals, about his orb; producing certain stable energies, and advancing backwards and forwards: (terms by which the skilful in the spherical theory signify such like phenomena of the stars) to which we may add, as manifest to every one, that the light of the moon is augmented or diminished according to her distance from the sun.

Is it not then highly probable, that the ordination of the intellectual Gods, which is more ancient than that of bodies, is analogous to the mundane disposition? Hence we infer his perfective power from the whole phenomena, because he gives vision to visive natures; for he perfects these by his light. But we collect his demiurgic and prolific power from the mutation of the universe; and his capacity of connecting all things into one, from the properties of motion conspiring into union and consent; and middle position, from his own central situation. Lastly, we infer his royal establishment among the intellectual Gods, from his middle order between the planets; for if we perceived these, or as many other properties, belonging to any other of the apparent Gods, we should not ascribe the principality among the Gods to the sun. But if he has nothing in common with the rest, except that beneficent power which he imparts to all, we ought to rely on the testimony of the Cyprian priests, who raised common altars to Jupiter and the Sun; or, indeed, prior to these, we should confide in Apollo, who is the attendant of this God; for thus he speaks: Jupiter, Pluto, Serapis, and the Sun, are one. And thus we should consider that there is a common, or rather one and the same principality, among the intellectual Gods, of Jupiter and the Sun; hence as it appears to me, Plato does not absurdly call Pluto a prudent God; whom we also denominate Serapis, as if he were ἀιδῆσ, i.e. invisible and intellectual; to whom, according to his relation, the souls of those are elevated who have lived most wisely and just. For we must not conceive a Pluto of that kind, such as fables describe, horrid to the view; but one benevolent and mild, who perfectly liberates souls from the bands of generation, and fixes such as are not liberated in other bodies, that he may punish them for their guilt, and absolve the decisions of justice. Add too, that he likewise leads souls on high, and elevates them to the intelligible world.

But that this is not a recent opinion, but embraced by the most ancient of poets, Homer and Hesiod, whether this arose the conceptions of their minds, or whether from a divine afflatus, as is usual with poets, enthusiastically energizing about truth, is evident from hence: for the one describing the genealogy of the sun, says, that he descended from Hyperion and Thea, that he may by this means evince, that he is the legitimate progeny of the super-eminent God; for how can we otherwise interpret the epithet Hyperion? And as to what pertains to the appellation Thea, is he not, after another mode, denominated by this means the most divine of beings? Nor must we conceive, with respect to his nature, that there is any copulation of bodies, or intervention of nuptials, which are the incredible and paradoxical sports of the poetic muse; but we must believe that his father and generator is most divine and supreme: and such will he be, who is above all things, about whom all things are placed, and for whose sake all things subsist. But Homer denominates him Hyperion from his father, that he may evince his perfect freedom and his superiority over all necessity: for Jupiter, who, as he says, is the lord of all, compels others to his will; but to this divinity, who threatened, on account of the impiety of Ulysses' companions, to forsake Olympus, he does not say,

"I heave the Gods, the ocean, and the land;"

nor does he menace chains or the exertion of force; but promises vengeance on the authors of this impiety, and entreats him to continue to illuminate the Gods. What else then can he mean to insinuate by this narration, but that this deity, exclusive of his perfect freedom, is of a telesiurgic nature, or is endued with a perfective operative power? For why would the Gods require his assistance, unless by occultly illuminating their essence and being, he obtained a power of accomplishing the goods we have previously described? For when Homer says,

Meantime, unwearied with his heavenly way,
In ocean's waves the' unwilling light of day
Quenched his red orb, at Juno's high command,

he indicates nothing more than that a premature opinion of night arose, through the intervention of horrid darkness: for of this Goddess the poet thus speaks in another place:

> Illustrious Juno then before them spread
> A mist profound.--------------------------

But we shall take our leave of the poets, because they mingle much of human imperfection with the excellence of divinity; however, what this deity appears to have taught concerning himself and others, we shall now endeavor to unfold.

The region surrounding this earth has its being entirely in generation, or in an ever flowing subsistence. Who is it then that confers perpetuity on its nature? Is it not he, who comprehends it in limited measures! For the nature of body cannot be infinite; since it is neither without generation nor self subsistent: but if any thing should be continually produced from an apparent existence, without being resolved into it again, the essence of things in generation would be no more. Hence the solar God, exciting a nature of this kind with a sure and measured motion, raises and invigorates it as he approaches, and diminishes and destroys it as he recedes; or rather he vivifies it by his progress, moving and pouring into generation the rivers of life. But when he deserts one hemisphere and is transferred into another, he brings destruction on corruptible natures. And, indeed, the communication of good, originating from this divinity, equally diffuses itself on the earth: for it is participated by different regions at different periods; so that generation will never fail, nor will the God confer his beneficence on the passive world with any variations of good: for as there is a sameness of essence, so likewise of energy among the Gods; especially in the sun, the king of the universe, whose motion is the most simple of all the natures, revolving contrary to the course of the world. And it is by this argument that the illustrious Aristotle proves his superiority to the rest: but a power by no means obscure is imparted to the world from the other intellectual Gods. What then? Are we to exclude these while we confer sovereignty on the sun? By no means; for we endeavor to procure credibility, concerning unapparent essences, from such as are manifest and known. Hence, as he gives perfection, and harmonizes both to himself and to the universe, the power proceeding from the rest, and diffused on the earth, so it is proper to believe, that in the secret recesses of their natures they have a conjunction with each other; the sun, indeed, possessing the principality, while the rest conspire into union and consent with his divinity.

But as we have asserted that he is allotted a middle situation between the middle intellectual Gods, what this middle station may be, in the midst of which he is established, may the sovereign sun enable me to explain. By a medium, therefore, in this place, we mean not that which is observed in contraries, and is equally distant from the extremes; as among colors, yellow, between white and black; or warmth, between heat and cold, and others of a similar nature; but that which unifies and copulates things divided and separate; such as is the harmony of Empedocles, from which he perfectly excluded strife and contention. What then are the natures which he connects, and of which he is said to be the medium? We reply, that he is the unifying medium of the apparent and mundane deities, and of the immaterial and intelligible Gods, who surround the Good; as he is an intelligible and divine essence multiplied without passivity, and augmented without addition. After this manner, then, the intellectual and all-beautiful essence of the royal sun, consists from no temperament of the extremes, but is perfect and free from all mixture, both of apparent and invisible, of sensible and intelligible Gods. And thus we have declared the medium which it is proper to ascribe to his nature.

But if it be requisite to be more explicit, and to explain the medium of his essence, and how we may separately, and by species, understand his proportion to the first and last, though it is difficult to accomplish the whole of this arduous undertaking, yet we will attempt the explanation to the best of our ability. There is, then, an intelligible one perpetually pre-existent, who comprehends the universality of things in one. But what? Is not the whole world one animal, profoundly replenished with soul and intellect, and perfect from the conjunction of perfect parts? Hence, between this twofold unifying perfection, I mean that which in the intelligible place comprehends all things in one, and the other which is conversant about the world, and coalesces in one and the same perfect nature, the unifying perfection of the royal sun intervenes, seated in the midst of the intellectual Gods. But, posterior to this, there is a certain connection of the Gods in the intelligible world, harmonizing all things into one; for do not the heavens appear to revolve about the substance of the fifth body, which connects all their parts, and binds and establishes in itself their mutually dissoluble and flowing natures? Hence the royal sun so collects into one these two connecting essences, one of which is perceived in intelligibles, but the other in sensibles, that he perfectly imitates the connecting power in intellectuals, of which he is the source. But he presides and rules over that last unifying nature which is perceived about this apparent world. And I know not whether that which is called self-subsistent, which is first among intelligibles, but last in the celestial phenomena, possesses the middle, self-subsistent essence of the royal sun; from which first-operative' substance that splendor emanates which illumines every thing in the apparent world.

Again, that we may consider this affair in a different mode, since there is one demiurges of the universe, but many demiurgic Gods, who revolve round the heavens, it is proper to place in the midst of these the mundane administration of the sun: besides, the fertile power of life is copious and redundant in intelligibles, and the world is full of the same prolific life. Hence it is evident that the fertile life of the sovereign sun is a medium between the two, as the mundane phenomena perpetually evince. For, with respect to forms, some he perfects, and others he fabricates; some he adorns, and others he excites; nor is any thing capable of advancing into light and generation without the demiurgic power of the sun. Besides this, if we attend to the sincere, pure, and immaterial essence of intelligibles, to which nothing extrinsically flows, and nothing foreign adheres, but which is full of its own domestic simplicity, and afterwards consider the defecated nature of that pure and divine body which is conversant with mundane bodies revolving in an orb, and which is free from all elementary mixture, we shall find that the splendid and incorruptible essence of the royal sun, is a medium between the immaterial purity of intelligibles and that which in sensibles is sincere and remote from generation and corruption. But the greatest argument for the truth of this is derived from hence, that the light which flows from the sun upon the earth will not suffer itself to be mingled with any thing; nor is it polluted by any sordid nature, or by any contagion; but it abides every where pure, undefiled, and impassive. Again, if we consider not only immaterial, and intelligible forms, but such as are sensible, subsisting in matter, the middle intellectual situation of forms about the mighty sun will be no less certain and clear: for these afford continual assistance to forms merged in matter; so that they could neither exist, nor preserve themselves in existence, unless this beneficent deity co-operated with their essence. In short, is he not the cause of the secretion of forms and the concretion of matter? from whom we not only possess the power of understanding his nature, but from whom our eyes are endued with the faculty of sight? for the distribution of rays throughout the world, and union of light, exhibit the demiurgic secretion of the artificer.

But as there are many apparent goods in the essence of this divinity which demonstrate his middle position between the intelligible and mundane Gods, let us pass on to the last and apparent condition of the sun. His first condition then about the last world is, that of the solar angels, whose idea and hypostasis is situated in their paradigm or exemplar. But, posterior to this, his power generative of sensibles succeeds; whose more honorable part contains the cause of the heavens and the stars, and whose inferior part presides over generation, at the same time comprehending eternally in itself an essence invariably the same. But indeed no one can explain all that is contained in the essence of this God, though intelligence should be conferred on him by this divinity himself; since intellect appears to me incapable of comprehending the whole.

It will here however be proper to set a seal, as it were, to our much-extended oration, that we may pass on to other disquisitions, which require a contemplation by no means inferior to the former: but what this seal may be, and what the conception of his essence, who summarily comprehends the universality of things, may the God himself inform my understanding; as I am desirous of comprehending with brevity from what principle he proceeds, in what his nature consists, and with what goods he replenishes the apparent world. We must assert, therefore, that from one God, I mean from one intelligible world, one sovereign sun proceeds, constituted in the middle of the intellectual Gods, according to an all-various mediocrity; who connecting concordant and friendly natures, and such as, though distant, conspire into friendship and consent, conciliates in unity first natures with the last; containing in himself the middle of perfection, and connection of prolific life and uniform essence: who, besides this, is the author of every good to the sensible world, not only illuminating and adorning it by his splendor, but giving the same subsistence with himself to the essence of solar angels, and comprehending an unbigoted cause of generated natures; and, prior to this, containing a cause of eternal bodies free from the depredations of age, and endued with stability of life.

And thus far our oration has extended concerning the essence of the God; in which, though we have omitted many things, we have delivered not a few. But because the copiousness of his powers, and the beauty of his energies, are so great, that the properties considered in his essence vehemently excel: (for such is the condition of divine natures, that when they proceed into apparent form, they are multiplied through a redundancy and fecundity of life,) consider what occasion there is, that we who are as yet scarcely refreshed from the preceding long oration, should venture on an immense ocean of enquiry. Let us, however, dare the investigation, trusting in the assistance of the God, and endeavor to accomplish our discourse.

In the first place, then, we must consider that whatever we have previously asserted concerning his essence, belongs in common to his powers; for the essence of the God is not one thing, his power another, and his energy a third; since all that he wishes, he both is, and can be, and produces in energy: for neither does he wish to be that which he is not, nor is he unable to become what he wishes, nor does he wish to energize what he cannot effect. The case indeed is very different with respect to mankind; for in man a twofold and discordant nature is discerned conciliated into one, i.e. the nature of soul and body; the former of which is divine, and the latter shadowy and dark, the source of contention and strife. Hence, as Aristotle observes, neither pleasures nor grief are in amicable conjunction with our nature; for what is pleasant to the one procures molestation to its contrary, the other. But among the Gods nothing of this kind subsists; for their essence supplies them with good, invariably, and in a perpetual series. Whatever therefore we have asserted for the purpose of explaining his essence, the same must be applied to his powers and energies. But since our oration appears to reciprocate in these, it follows that we must consider in our subsequent speculations about his powers and energies, that these are not his operations only, but his essence: for there are certain divinities allied to, and connate with, the sun, who augment the pure essence of the God, and who, though they are multiplied in the world, yet subsist uniformly about the sun. But attend, in the first place, to their assertions who have not contemplated the heavens, like horses, or oxen, or other irrational and brutal animals, but have labored to investigate an unapparent nature from sensible appearances. And prior to this, you may, if so inclined, speculate a little concerning his supermundane powers and energies. Of these powers, the first is that by which he causes the whole of an intellectual essence to appear profoundly one, by collecting extremes into one and the same; for as we clearly perceive in the sensible world that air and water are situated between fire and earth, for the purpose of connecting the extremes as by a bond, there is no reason why we should not admit a similar establishment in an essence prior to body and separate from its nature; which obtains the principle of generation, and is itself superior to origin.

Hence, in an essence of this kind, as well as among elementary forms, the extreme principles which are separated from all corporeal commerce being through certain mediums collected into one by the royal sun, become united about his nature: and with this indeed the demiurgic power of Jupiter accords; to whom, as we have previously related, temples were dedicated in Cyprus in common with the sun. In the same place, too, we have brought the testimony of Apollo in confirmation of its truth, who doubtless understands his nature better than the wisest of mankind; for he is present and communicates with the sun, possessing the same simplicity of intellection, stability of essence, and sameness of energy. For Apollo appears by no means to separate from the sun the multiplied and partial operation of Bacchus, but rather, as he perpetually subjects him to the sun, and demonstrates him to be his attendant, he assists us in framing the most beautiful conceptions about the God. Besides, so far as the sun contains in himself the principles of the most beautiful intellectual temperament, he becomes Apollo, the leader of the Muses; but so far as he accomplishes the elegant order of the whole of life, he generates Esculapius in the world; whom at the same time he comprehended in himself prior to the world.

But though we may contemplate many powers of the God, yet we can never exhaust the whole. This, however, ought to suffice us, that in a nature separate from, and more ancient than, body, and in a genus of causes abstracted from appearances, we may contemplate an equal, and the same principality and power of Jupiter and the sun. We may likewise survey a simplicity of intelligence, together with perpetuity, and a stability of sameness, united with Apollo; but divisibility of operation, in conjunction with Bacchus, who presides over a partial essence. Add to, that we may perceive the power of beautiful symmetry and intellectual temperament in union with Musagetes. And lastly, we may conceive that power which fills up the elegant order of the whole of life as combined with Esculapius. And thus much concerning the supermundane powers of the God; whose correspondent operations above the apparent world consist in diffusing a perpetual plenitude of good; for as he is the genuine progeny of the Good, from whom he receives a perfect and beneficent condition, he distributes this excellence of his nature to all the intellectual Gods, assigning them an essence benignant and perfect. But another employment of the God consists in conferring an absolute distribution of intelligible beauty among intellectual and incorporeal forms; for as the generative essence apparent in nature desires to beget in the beautiful and to expose its progeny to the light, it is necessary that an essence should antecede and be the leader of this, which eternally generates in intelligible beauty: at the same time we must observe that it does not operate at one time and not at another; or beget at one period and become afterwards barren; for whatever is sometimes beautiful here, is perpetually fair among intelligible natures. Hence we must assert, that an unbigoted progeny, subsisting in intellectual and eternal beauty, antecedes every prolific cause in the apparent world: and this progeny the sun contains, and establishes about his own essence; conferring on him a perfect intellect, and by this means giving sight, as it were, to his eyes by the benefit of his light. In a similar manner, in the intelligible world, by means of an intellectual paradigm, which scatters a light far brighter than ethereal splendor, he extends, as it appears to me, the power of intellection, and of being intelligible, to all intellectual natures. But, besides this, there is another admirable energy belonging to the sun, the king of the universe; I mean that better condition which he attributes to the more excellent genera of beings, such as angels, Daemons, Heroes, and partial souls, who perpetually abide in the reason of their exemplar and idea without merging themselves in the darkness of body. And thus we have hastily explained, to the best of our ability, the supermundane essence of the God, by celebrating its powers and operations in that universal king the sun. But since the eyes (as it is said) are more worthy of belief than the ears, though they deserve less credibility, and are more imbecile than intelligence, let us now consider his apparent fabrication, having first entreated his pardon, for endeavoring, with moderate abilities, to celebrate his divinity.

The apparent world then, perpetually subsists about the sun; and his light, which surrounds the universe, obtains an eternal seat; so as not to be subject to any variations of place, since it is for ever the same. But if any one is willing to conceive by mere thought alone this eternal nature as temporal, he will easily know respecting the sun, the king of the universe, who immediately illuminates every thing with his light, what abundant goods he eternally confers on the world. I am not indeed ignorant that both the great Plato, and Jamblichus of Chalcis, who was posterior to Plato in time, though not in the powers of mind, and to whose books I am indebted for other philosophical information, as well as the present arcana, consider the sun as generated for hypothesis only; and establish a certain temporal production for the sake of disputation, that we may be able to comprehend the magnitude of his effects. But this is on no account to be attempted by me, who am inferior to them in all mental endowments; especially since the very hypothesis of his temporary production is not without danger, as was evident to that illustrious Hero Jamblichus himself. However, since this God proceeded from an eternal cause, or rather produced all things from eternity, generating such as are apparent at present from unapparent causes, by a divine will, an ineffable celerity, and an invincible power: hence he is allotted the middle region of the heavens, as more accommodated to his nature, that he may afford to the Gods, produced from, and together with him, an equal distribution of good; and besides this, that he may preside over the eight spheres of the heavens; and may govern the ninth fabrication, which possesses an eternal vicissitude in generation and decay. For as to the planets, it is manifest, that, dancing, as it were, round the sun, their motions are measured by a certain symphony of figures with respect to the God; to which we may add, that the whole heavens harmonizing with him in all their parts, are replenished with Gods from his divinity: for this God presides over the five celestial orbs, and by revolving round three of these, generates as many Graces, while the rest are called the balances of mighty Necessity. But these observations are perhaps more obscure to the Greeks, and on that account unacceptable; as if we should relate nothing but what is common and known.

But indeed they are by no means unusual and strange; for who (O ye most wise, and without inquiry assenting to a multitude of assertions) are the Dioscuri? Are they not said to live on alternate days, because it is not lawful for both of them to be apparent on the same day; as, for instance, that you may clearly understand me, yesterday and today? Then again, consider with respect to the same Dioscuri, endeavoring with me to adapt your conceptions to their nature, lest we should assert any thing new and unintelligible. But indeed we shall find nothing of this kind, though we scrutinize in the most accurate manner: for the assertion of some theologists that they are the two hemispheres of the world, by no means pertains to the present investigation; since it is not easy to conceive why each of these is called ετερημερος, or diurnally alternate, as their illustration is gradually augmented without any sensation of diurnal increment.

But we are now entering upon speculations, in the course of which we may possibly appear to make some innovations. In the first place then, those may be very properly said to participate the same day, to whom an equal time of the solar progression, in one and the same month, belongs. Let any one now consider how this diurnal alternation can be accommodated, as well with other, as the tropical circles. But a speculation of this kind is not indeed adapted to our present investigation; because these circles are always apparent, and are conspicuous to the inhabitants of regions situated in opposite shadows, each to each; yet he who perceives the one cannot by any means discover the other. However, that we may not dwell any longer in explaining the present affair, the sun, as we know by his annual revolutions, is the parent of the seasons; and considered as never receding from the poles, he is the Ocean, the ruler of a two-fold essence; nor is such an assertion by any means obscure, since Homer, so long before us, calls Ocean the generation of mortals, of the blessed divinities, and of all things: and this indeed with the greatest truth and propriety; for there is nothing in the universe which is not the natural progeny of the Ocean. But are you willing I should explain in what respect this concerns the vulgar? Though perhaps it might be better to be silent, I will speak on this occasion: I will speak, though my discourse will not be properly received by all.

The solar orb, then, is moved in the starless, which is far higher then the inerratic sphere. Hence, he is not the middle of the planets, but of the three worlds, according to the mystic hypotheses; if it be proper to call them hypotheses, and not rather dogmatic; confining the appellation of hypothesis to the doctrine of the sphere: for the truth of the former is testified by men who audibly received this information from Gods, or mighty Daemons; but the latter is founded on the probability arising from the agreement of the phenomena. Hence, if any one should esteem it better both to praise and confide in the former, such a one, whether I am trifling or in earnest, will meet with my esteem and admiration.

But besides those which I have mentioned, there is an innumerable multitude of celestial Gods, perceived by such as do not contemplate the heavens indolently and after the manner of brutes. As the sun quadruply divides these three worlds, on account of the communion of the zodiac with each, so he again divides the zodiac into twelve powers of Gods, and each of these into three others, so that thirty-six are produced in the whole. Hence, as it appears to me, a triple benefit of the Graces proceeds to us from the heavens, I mean from those circles which the God quadruply dividing produces in consequence of this, a quadripartite beauty and elegance of seasons and times. But the Graces also imitate a circle in their resemblances on the earth. Add too, that Bacchus is the source of joy, who is said to obtain a common kingdom with the sun. But why should I here mention the epithet Horus, or other names of the Gods, all of which correspond with the divinity of the sun? Mankind, indeed, may conceive the excellence of the God from his operations; since he perfects the heavens with intellectual goods, and renders them partakers of intelligible beauty. For as he originates from this beauty, he applies himself, both totally and by parts, to the distribution of good . . . . These Gods indeed preside over all motion, as far as to the utmost boundaries of the world; so that both nature and soul, and every thing that exists, is perfected by their beneficent communications. But the sun combining this abundant army of Gods into one ruling unity, confers on it the providence of Minerva; who originated, according to fables, from the head of Jupiter; but who, according to our opinion, proceeded from the whole of the sovereign sun, and is wholly comprehended in his nature. Hence we differ from fables in this, that we do not consider her as springing from the summit, but as totally born from the whole of Jupiter; for by conceiving no difference between Jupiter and the sun, we shall think agreeable to the decisions of the ancients. And, indeed, by calling the sun providential Minerva, we shall not assert any thing new, if we properly understand the following verse. "he came to Python, and to providential Minerva." For thus the ancients seated Minerva with Apollo, who appears to differ in nothing from the sun. And I know not whether Homer, by a certain divine instinct, (for it is probable that he was seized with a divine fury,) prophesies this, when he sings,

> So might my life, and glory know no bound,
> Like Pallas worshiped, like the Sun renowned.

That is to say, like Jupiter, who is the same with the sun. And as the king Apollo, on account of his simplicity of intellection, communicates with the sun, so likewise it is proper to believe that Minerva, since she receives her essence from this deity, and is his perfect intellection, combines into union, without any confusion, the Gods who surround the sovereign sun; and that the same Goddess, from the summit of heaven, pours through the seven planetary orbs, as far as to the moon, the genuine and pure rivers of life; indeed she fills the moon, who is the last of the orbicular bodies, with intelligence; and thus causes her to contemplate the intelligibles above the heavens, to regard inferior natures, and to beautify matter with the investiture of forms, by removing from its shadowy essence whatever it contains, wild, turbulent, and destitute of order.

But the goods which Minerva confers on mankind are wisdom, intelligence, and operative arts: she is also said to obtain the towers of cities, because she establishes civil community by her wisdom. It is likewise proper to declare a few particulars respecting Venus, who, according to the learned among the Phoenicians, (which is likewise my opinion) has a demiurgic community with Minerva. Venus, then, is the temperament of the celestial Gods, and the friendship and union, by which their harmony subsists; for as she is proximate to the sun, in conjunction with whom she revolves, she fills the heavens with the best temperament, gives fertility to the earth, and is the source of perpetuity to the generation of animals. And of all this the sovereign sun is the primary cause: but Venus concurs in her operations with this divinity; alluring our souls with pleasure, and diffusing from ether, delightful and incorruptible splendors on the earth, far superior to the brightest refulgence of gold. I am likewise desirous of disclosing a few arcana from the Phoenician theology; whether or not in vain, our oration will gradually disclose. Those, then, who inhabit Edessa, a region eternally dedicated to the sun, consider Monimus, and Azizus, as the attendants of this deity; Monimus, according to Jamblichus, (from whom we have received a few observations out of many,) being the same with Mercury and Azizus, the same as Mars; and each of them, in conjunction with the sun, diffusing a variety of goods on the earth.

Such, then, are the effects of this God in the heavens, and through these his perfections are propagated to the utmost boundaries of the earth: but as it would be arduous to enumerate all his operations beneath the moon, let us celebrate them by a compendious recital. I know, indeed, that I have already mentioned these, when I investigated the invisible properties of the God from the phenomena; but the order of my discourse requires that I should now resume the narration.

As therefore we have asserted that the sun obtains the principality among the intellectual Gods, whose indivisible essence is surrounded with a great and uniform multitude of Gods, as likewise that he is the leader and lord of the natures, which among sensibles revolve in an orb, with an eternal and blessed progression; and that as he fills the heavens with apparent splendor, so likewise with an infinite abundance of unapparent goods; from whose occult and divine energy too the goods derived from the other apparent Gods receive their perfection; so likewise we must consider; that certain Gods reside in the receptacle of generation, who are comprehended by the sovereign sun, and who governing the quadruple nature, are established about the souls of the elements, together with the three genera, more excellent than man. But consider what mighty goods he confers on partial souls! For to these he extends judgment, governs them by justice, and purifies them by his splendor. Besides this, does he not move and suscitate all nature, by imparting to it fecundity from on high? For he is the true cause of particular natures arriving at the destined end of their existence; since (as Aristotle observes) man and the sun generate man. Hence, we should form the same judgment, of the sovereign sun, in every other effect of particular natures: for does not the God fabricate for us rains and winds, and whatever else is produced in the aerial regions? Since, by giving heat to the earth he excites vapor and fume, by means of which, not only these sublime phenomena, but likewise subterranean events of greater or less importance, are produced.

But why should we protract this enumeration any farther, since it is now proper to hasten to the conclusion; first of all celebrating the goods which the sun bestows on mankind? For as he is the source of our existence, so likewise of the aliment by which that existence is supported. And indeed he confers on us more divine advantages peculiar to souls; for he loosens these from the bands of a corporeal nature, reduces them to the kindred essence of divinity, and assigns them the subtile and firm texture of divine splendor, as a vehicle in which they may safely descend to the realms of generation. And these benefits of the God have been celebrated by others according to their desert, and require the assent of faith more than the evidence of demonstration.

But we ought not to fear attempting the relation of such things as are naturally the objects of knowledge to all men. Plato, then, asserts that the heavens are the masters of wisdom to mankind, since it is from these that we learn the nature of number; and our knowledge of its diversity is solely derived from the revolution of the sun. To which Plato also adds, that the heavens, by the succession of many days and nights, never cease to instruct the dullest apprehensions in the art of numbering; and that this is also effected by the varying light of the moon, which is solely imparted to this Goddess from the sun; indeed the farther we advance in our researches into wisdom of this kind, the more shall we every where perceive the symphony and consent of other deities with the sun. And this Plato himself evinces when he says, that the Gods pitying the human race, which is naturally laborious and afflicted, gave to us Bacchus and the Muses, who perpetually combine in one harmonious choir. But the sun appears to be the common ruler of these, since he is celebrated as the father of Bacchus, and the leader of the Muses; for does not Apollo, whose government is united in amicable conjunction with these divinities, diffuse his oracles over all the earth? Does he not extend divinely-inspired wisdom to mankind, and adorn cities with sacred and political institutions? It is this divinity who, through the colonies of the Greeks, has civilized the greatest part of the globe, and disposed it to receive with less reflectance the authority of the Romans; who indeed are not only descended from a Grecian origin, but have adopted, and perpetually preserved, from the beginning to the end, the sacred rites of the Greeks, and their piety towards the Gods. To which we may add, that the Romans have established a form of government by no means inferior to that of any of the cities which have enjoyed the best constitutions, but rather one excelling all the modes of political administration which have ever been adopted. And through these considerations, I consider the city of Rome as Grecian, both on account of its origin, and political institutions. But why, besides this, should I assert to you, how the sun, by generating Esculapius, has provided for the health and safety of all things? And how he imparts all-various virtue, while he sends to mankind Venus and Minerva in amicable conjunction? Like a provident guardian appointing, by immutable law, that the mixed nature of bodies should pursue no other end than the generation of its like. Hence, by the constant revolutions of this deity, all vegetable and animal tribes are excited to the propagation of natures similar to their own. Why again is it necessary, to celebrate the rays and light of the sun? For who does not perceive the dreadful aspect of the night, which is not illustrated either by the splendor of the moon or stars? So that from this circumstance alone, we may conjecture how great a good we obtain through the light derived from this resplendent God. But this light indeed he imparts perpetually, and without being interrupted by the intervening shades of night, to places where it is necessary, or the regions above the moon; but to us he benignantly affords a cessation from labor, through the friendly interposition of the night. Indeed there would be no bound to our oration if we should pursue every particular of this kind, since there is no good belonging to our existence which we do not receive as the gift of this divinity; whether it is perfectly imparted from him alone, or receives its consummation from him, through the ministry of other Gods.

But this deity presides over the city of Rome, and on this account Jupiter, the celebrated father of all things, not only resides in its tower, together with Minerva, and Venus, but Apollo also resides on the Palatine hill, together with the sun himself, who is universally known to be the same with Apollo. But I will mention a few things out of a many, principally pertaining to the sun, and to us who are the descendants of Romulus, and Aeneas. For Aeneas, according to tradition, descended from Venus, who assists the operations of the sun, and is allied to his nature: and the son of Mars is reported to have been the founder of our city; which, however paradoxical and incredible, was abundantly confirmed by succeeding prodigies. However, as I am well aware, and have already mentioned, that Mars, who is called by the Edessenian Syrians, Azizus, is the forerunner of the sun, I shall not insist on this particular at present. But it may be asked, why is a wolf consecrated to Mars rather than to the sun? For they denominate from hence the space of a year Lycabas. Nor is this appellation assumed by Homer only, and the more illustrious Greeks, but by a God himself; for thus he speaks: "Accomplishing, by a leaping progression, Lycabas, the path of twelve months."

Are you willing therefore that I should demonstrate by a more powerful argument, that the founder of our city not only descended from Mars, but that however the martial, and noble Daemon, who is said to have met with Silvia carrying the bath of the Goddess, might contribute to the fabrication of his body, yet the soul of the God Quirinus wholly proceeded from the sun? For we ought, I think, to believe in general report. As therefore the conjunction of the sun and moon, who distribute in common the principality of apparent natures, sent his soul on the earth, so likewise this conjunction received it back again from earth into the heavens, after it had consumed by the fire of thunder whatever was mortal in his corporeal frame. And from hence it is evident that the demiurgic Goddess of terrene concerns, who is in a most perfect manner subjected to the sun, received our Quirinus, when he was sent by providential Minerva on the earth; and afterwards brought him back, when flying from. this terrene abode, to the sun, the sovereign of the world. But if you are desirous, besides this, that I should employ another argument on the same subject, derived from the works of King Numa, behold the unextinguished fire, enkindled from the sun which is preserved among us by sacred virgins according to the different seasons of the year; and which, by this means, imitates the beneficent energy of the moon in her revolution round the earth.

But I am able to produce another, and a much more indubitable argument, concerning this God, from the institutions of that most divine king. For while all other nations number their months from the course of the moon, we alone, together with the Egyptians, measure the days of our year from the revolutions of the sun. To all which, if I should add that we celebrate Mithras, and institute quadrennial contests in honor of the sun, I should speak of things more recent and known: but it will be better perhaps to adduce one testimony from more ancient traditions.

Different nations then differently determine the commencement of the annual circuit; for some reckon from the vernal equinox; some from the middle of summer; most from autumn in its decline: yet all these celebrate the most apparent gifts of the sun. For some with grateful recollection honor the God for the opportunity afforded them in autumn for rustic labor; when the earth, pouring from her kindly womb all-various fruits, is clothed with fertility, and every where exhibits the appearance of splendid hilarity; when the sea smoothes its waters for the convenience of navigation; and the stormy brow of winter is changed into festive serenity.

But others derive the origin of their year from the summer day; because at that time they have greater security with respect to the success of fruits; since the various seeds deposited in the earth are at that period collected together; apples are in their most flourishing state; and the depending fruit of trees has acquired maturity through the benevolent heat of the solar fire. But others more elegant than these, establish the end of the year, when every fruit has acquired its most perfect vigor, and is tending to decay; and on this account, when autumn is in its decline, they date the commencement of their year. But our ancestors having learned from that most divine King Numa, to be more studious in venerating this divinity than other nations, without paying so much attention to what is useful, (acting in this respect in a manner becoming men of a divine nature and excellent understanding) directed their attention rather to the cause of these effects, and commanded the people to bind their heads at that period of the year, when the sun, having left the last meridian limit, returns to us again, and bending his course towards Capricorn, as to his destined goal, proceeds from the south to the north, that he may impart, by such a progression, his annual benefits to mankind. And from hence we may conjecture, that an attentive consideration of this particular induced our ancestors to establish this period as the beginning of the year; for they do not perform this annual ceremony on the day in which the sun commences his revolution, but when his progression from the meridian to the north is universally apparent: for as yet the subtlety of those canons was not sufficiently known, which were discovered by the Chaldeans and Egyptians, and perfected by Hipparchus and Ptolomy. But forming their judgment solely from the testimony of the senses, they pursued the celestial phenomena:

those of a more modern period, perceiving at the same time the rectitude of their observations. Hence, immediately on the close of the last month, which is dedicated to Saturn, and prior to the beginning of the new year, we celebrate most magnificent games in honor of the sun, whom we denominate unconquered; and, in conjunction with these games, it is unlawful to exhibit any of those sorrowful spectacles which necessarily pertain to the last month of the year.

But after the Saturnalia, which are the last of all, the Helian ceremonies return with the revolving year. And I sincerely wish that the sovereign Gods would frequently permit me to celebrate and engage in these sacred festivals, and particularly that the sun, the king of the universe, would grant me permission, who from eternity is produced about the prolific essence of the Good, as a harmonizing medium, between the middle intellectual Gods; on whom he confers indissoluble connection, infinite beauty, affluent fecundity, perfect intellect, and an eternal accumulation of every good: who, in an indivisible moment, illuminates his conspicuous seat, which he eternally obtains in the middle region of the heavens: who imparts his intellectual beauty to this visible universe, and fills all the celestial regions with as many Gods as he comprehends intellectually in himself, multiplied indivisibly about him, and uniformly conjoined with his essence. Nor does he less comprehend in his divinity the sublunary region, through a perpetuity of generation, and a communication of goods derived through a circular body; at the same time extending his providential care to the whole human race, and privately protecting the city of Rome. To which I may add, that he has generated my soul from eternity, and rendered it an attendant on his divinity. May he, therefore, communicate these gifts, and such others as we have already earnestly implored him to impart. But may he bestow on our city in common a perpetual duration, and benevolently preserve it from hostile devastation. And lastly, may he confer upon me, so long as he shall supply the streams of life, felicity and prosperity in whatever pertains to human and divine concerns: but may I live, and administer public affairs, as long as shall be pleasing to his divinity, useful to myself, and advantageous to the common affairs of the Romans.

And such, dear Sallust, is the oration, which, being mostly composed in the space of three nights, according to the triple administration of the God, and from the suggestions of memory at the time, I have dared to submit to your inspection; since a former piece of my composition on the Saturnalia, did not appear to you entirely foreign from the purpose, and undeserving your esteem. But if you are desirous of more perfect, and mystic discourses on this subject, by revolving the books of the divine Jamblichus, composed with the same design as the present oration, you will find the perfect consummation of human wisdom. But may the mighty sun, nevertheless, enable me to understand whatever pertains to his divinity; and to impart my information to all men in common, and privately to those who are worthy of such instruction. In the mean time, till the God shall crown my desires in this respect with success, let us both venerate Jamblichus, the friend of this divinity, from whom we have committed to writing a few particulars out of many which occurred to our recollection at the time: for I well know that no one can speak more perfectly on this subject than Jamblichus; though by the most vigorous contention, he should endeavor to add something of novelty to his discourse; for by such an attempt, as it is reasonable to suppose, he would deviate from true conceptions of the God.

Indeed if I had composed the present oration merely for the sake of instructing others, the labor of writing on such a theme after Jamblichus would perhaps have been in vain: but since I had no other intention than to render thanks to this divinity by a hymn, and considered my end accomplished in speaking of his essence to the utmost of my ability, I do not think that I have misspent my time by the present composition. For the admonition of Hesiod,

> Perform, according to your utmost power,
> Pure, sacred rites, to the immortal Gods.

is not only to be understood as necessary in sacrifices, but likewise in the praises of the Gods. In the third place, therefore, I earnestly entreat the sun, the king of the universe, that he will be propitious to me for my affection to his divinity; that he will impart to me a good life; more perfect wisdom; a divine intellect; and a gentle departure from the present state in a convenient time, that I may ascend to his divinity, and abide with him, if possible, in perpetual conjunction. But if this be a reward too great for my conduct on this terrene abode, may I at least be united with him for many, and long-extended periods of time.

Suggested Reading

- Adkins, Lesley and Roy A. Adkins. (1997) *Handbook to Life in Ancient Greece.*
- Alcaeus, Sappho, Athenaeus. *Greek Lyric I.* (trans) David A. Campbell.
- Anacreon, Anacreontea, Tzetzes. et al. *Greek Lyric II* (trans) David A. Campbell
- Archilochus, Aelius Aristides, Athenaeus, Hipponax, Plutarch, Semonides, et al. *Greek Iambic Poetry* (trans) Douglas E. Gerber.
- Aristotle. *The Complete Works of Aristotle.*
- Burkert, Walter. (1985) *Greek Religion.* (trans) John Raffan.
- Campbell, Drew. (2000) *Old Stones, New Temples*
- Carpenter, Thomas H. and Faraone, Christopher A. (1993) *Masks of Dionysus.*
- Cicero. *Cicero: Nature of the Gods: Academics.* (trans). H. Rackham.
- Dillon, John. (2003) *The Heirs of Plato: A Study of the Old Academy (347-274 BC).*
- Euripides. *Euripides: Children of Heracules, Hippolytus, Andromache, Hecuba.* (trans) Ed. David Kovacs.
- Flowers, Stephen Edred, Ph. D. (ed) (1995) *Hermetic Magic: The Postmodern Magical Papyrus of Abaris.*
- Garland, Robert. (1985) *The Greek Way of Death.*
- _____. (1990) *The Greek Way of Life.*
- Garrison, Daniel H. (2000) *Sexual Culture in Ancient Greece.*
- Godwin, David. (1992) *Light in Extension: Greek Magic from Homer to Modern Times.*
- Graf, Fritz, et al. Christopher A. Faraone and Dirk Obbink. (eds)

(1991) *Magika Hiera: Ancient Greek Magic & Religion.*

- Harrison, Jane Ellen. (1991) *Prolegomena: To the Study of Greek Religion.*
- Hesiod and Homer. *Homeric Hymns Epic Cycle Homerica.* (trans) H. G. Evelyn-White.
- Hippolyto. *The Dionysian Artificers.* (trans) Joseph da Costa.
- Homer. *The Odyssey.*
- _____. *Iliad.*
- Johnston, Sarah Iles. (1999) *Restless Dead: Encounters between the Living and the Dead in Ancient Greece.*
- Jones, Prudence & Nigel Pennick. (1995) *A History of Pagan Europe.*
- Kerenyi, Carl (1976) *Dionysos: Archetypal Image of Indestructible Life.*
- Lewis, H. Jeremiah. (2005) *A Temple of Words.*
- Mackenzie, Donald A. (1917) *Myths of Crete and Pre-Hellenic Europe.*
- Martin, Thomas R. (1996) *Ancient Greece: From Prehistoric to Hellenistic Times.*
- Menzies, Louisa. (1880) *Lives of the Greek Heroines.*
- Mikalson, Jon D. (1983) *Athenian Popular Religion.*
- _____. (1993) *Honor Thy Gods: Popular Religion in Greek Tragedy.*
- Meyer, Marvin W. (ed) (1986) *The Ancient Mysteries: A Sourcebook of Ancient Texts.*
- Nilsson, Martin P. (1940) *Greek Popular Religion.*
- Otto, Walter. (1965) *Dionysus: Myth and Cult.*
- Paris, Ginette. (1990) *Pagan Grace: Dionysos, Hermes, and Goddess Memory in Daily Life.*
- Parke, H. W. (1977) *Festivals of the Athenians.*
- Plato. *The Dialogues of Plato.*
- Reif, Jennifer. (1999) *Mysteries of Demeter: Rebirth of the Pagan Way.*
- Solon, Theognis, Tyrtaeus, et al. *Greek Elegiac Poetry: From the Seventh to the Fifth Centuries BC.* (trans) D. E. Gerber.
- Taylor, Thomas. (Trans) *The Hymns of Orpheus.*
- Telesco, Patricia (1996) *Seasons of the Sun: Celebrations from the World's Spiritual Traditions.*
- Willoughby, Harold R. (1929) *Pagan Regeneration A Study of Mystery Initiations in the Graeco-Roman World.*
- Winter, Sarah Kate Winter. (2004) *Kharis: Hellenic Polytheism Explored.*

About the Author

TIMOTHY JAY ALEXANDER was raised as a Roman Catholic but has been a practicing Pagan since 1985. He began his spiritual journey as a Solitary Wiccan, but found the religion did not truly reflect his spiritual beliefs. Beginning in 1991, Timothy started to self-identify as an Eclectic Pagan until in 2001, when he found his true spiritual path as a Hellenic Polytheistic Reconstructionist.

Timothy also owns and operates Mind-N-Magick.com, a Pagan and Wiccan search engine and directory that provides news, information, and services to the online Pagan Community. Mind-N-Maigck.com has been consistently rated the #1 Pagan search engine since 2005 by Alexa.com, and continually ranks in the top trafficked Pagan websites.

Timothy holds ordinations with both the Universal Life Church and the Church of Spiritual Humanism. He operates Alexander Ministries, a collection of ordained clergy providing services to those from minority religions and others in need of interfaith or customized ritual officiating.

Timothy is available to officiate weddings or to perform other ritual services in SE Pennsylvania. He can be contacted by visiting AlexanderMinistries.com.

Lightning Source UK Ltd.
Milton Keynes UK
UKHW041339061122
411712UK00012B/45